The Base String

The Underworld in Elizabethan Drama

Normand Berlin

Rutherford • Madison • Teaneck
FAIRLEIGH DICKINSON UNIVERSITY PRESS

Associated University Presses, Inc.
Cranbury, New Jersey 08512

6760
Printed in the United States of America

To my wife, Barbara

Acknowledgments

Anyone who writes on Elizabethan drama, especially on Shakespeare, must be indebted to all the scholars and critics who have come before him. The debt is paid in only a small way by acknowledgment in the footnotes, and there are many who do not receive even that small token of recognition. I would like to single out Bernard Spivack's *Shakespeare and the Allegory of Evil* as a particular help to me in my second chapter. (I am happy to note that Professor Spivack is now a colleague here at the University of Massachusetts.)

I have an unpayable debt to those teachers and advisers who have allowed me to "gladly lerne"—especially E. L. McAdam, Jr., John W. Knedler, Jr., and Richard Mallery at New York University; S. F. Johnson, Marjorie Hope Nicolson, Eric Bentley, and Maurice Valency at Columbia University; Travis Bogard, Willard Farnham, Bertrand Evans, and Alain

Renoir at the University of California, Berkeley. Professor Bogard advised me on the thesis from which this book stems, and Professor Johnson started me along the road to the underworld.

I would like to express my appreciation to the officers and staffs of The Folger Shakespeare Library, the New York Public Library, and the University of California Library at Berkeley for their facilities and assistance.

Warm thanks go to Thomas Yoseloff and Leslie Bialler for seeing the manuscript through its last stages.

My greatest debt is to my wife. Simply stated, without her the book could not have been written.

Amherst, Massachusetts—1967   N.B.

Contents

Introduction

When Hal asserts in *1 Henry IV* that he has "sounded the very base-string of humility," he is commenting both on his own behavior and on his relationship to the lower elements of society. The underworld, the base string of society, suggests to Hal the base string of humility; the plucking of one string produces the vibrations of another. This base string, the underworld, is vibrant not only for Hal but for many Elizabethan dramatists. It helped produce the music of Elizabethan life and drama.

The Elizabethan underworld deserves the attention of students of Elizabethan drama if only for its presence in so many plays. Its importance as an object of study, however, is based on qualitative, rather than quantitative, reasons. The underworld provides an image traditional enough and specific enough to allow one to focus clearly on the way the dramatist uses it; at the same time it provides an image rich enough to allow the dramatist to demonstrate his talents. The underworld is an interesting, and often significant, focus for understanding a particular dramatist's mind and art. Of course, it is only one focus. A partitioned study of a dramatist is by its very nature limited, because it places great emphasis on only one aspect of a total artistic effect. But until the complete critic comes along concentration on one aspect of a writer's work is a valid, and often effective, way to approach a dramatist, providing, of course, that the single aspect is related to the total meaning of the work under discussion. A unifying perspective, in this study the underworld, can often allow one to measure a dramatist's creative imagination with correctness and assurance.

Three dramatists—Dekker, Jonson, Shakespeare—have been selected for this study because they best exemplify the different uses the Elizabethan dramatists made of a part of society that demanded attention from them. Their treatment of the underworld will be discussed in the light of Elizabethan opinion concerning the underworld. It will be necessary, therefore, to investigate the literature that shaped this opinion and to examine the dramatic tradition that used the underworld before Dekker, Jonson, and Shakespeare put their plays on the boards. By knowing what the dramatists worked with one can best understand their essential worth and their unique contributions, if any. Chapters 1 and 2, therefore, will present the setting, while Chapters 3, 4, and 5 will investigate critically how the individual dramatists worked within that setting. The discussions of Dekker and Jonson will proceed according to the chronology of their plays. For Jonson a chronological approach is necessary because his use of the underworld indicates his development. For Dekker the chronological approach is as good an approach as any, because Dekker's art does not develop; it fluctuates with the demands of his audience. Proceeding chronologically is, in fact, useful in demonstrating Dekker's basic hack tendencies. Shakespeare, on the other hand, will be discussed according to the ways he uses the underworld, for this approach will indicate not only his development as an artist, but the full richness of his creative imagination.

The Base String

1

The Elizabethan Underworld:
Climate of Opinion

In sixteenth-century England, town and country were disturbed by a multitude of rogues and vagabonds. The cities, especially London, were filled with a variety of thieves eagerly looking for prey. The suburbs were infested with whores whose antics were both immoral and criminal. The roads between towns were harassed by highwaymen ready to stop any traveler to demand booty. To some, the activities of the underworld made Elizabethan England seem a dangerous place, where order and peace were constantly threatened; to others, a place of sin and gross immorality, where Jesus Christ was constantly betrayed. And there were those for whom the underworld made England a place of romance and excitement. Whatever view was held, the underworld was to be reckoned with—by the government, by the citizen, by the preacher, by the writer. It was a world, in short, that demanded attention from both Elizabethan playgoer and Elizabethan dramatist.

Many are the laws concerning the underworld that one finds in the statute-books from the reign of Henry VIII to the reign of Charles I.[1] That the underworld was an important segment of society can be discerned from a look at some of these statutes: ". . . there doe remayne yett in this Realme of England, specially about the Cittie of London, a great nomber of Ryffins and Vagabonds."[2] "And for because that within the citie of London, ther is at this present a great number of idle persons and masterles men . . ."[3] ". . . . all the partes of this Realme of England and Wales be presentlye with Roges Vacabonde and Sturdy Beggers excedinglye pestred, by means whereof daylye happeneth in the same Realme Murders, Thefte, and other greate Outrage . . ."[4]

Especially in Elizabeth's reign does the official literature indicate that the underworld is a serious menace to the whole community and a source of exasperation for the government, as the following letter to the Lord Mayor of London indicates:

Whereas wee have bin certified of many greevous and extra-ordinarie outrages committed of late by rogues, vagabondes and other licentious persons in diverse places not farr distant from the cittie of London, who have taken such boldnes as they are reported to assemble themselves and to have use of pistolles, petronelles or other peeces, therewith besetting the highe waies and doing much mischeefe in such riotous manner as the ordi-narie course of justice suffiseth not to keepe them in awe, and her Majesty's officers appointed for conservacion of the peace and punishment of such offendours are terrified with their vio-lence, as hath bin made knowen to us by the example of somme that have bin of late slaine and murthered in the pursuite of the said malefactours.[5]

Two years earlier a letter from Edward Hext, a justice of
the peace in Somersetshire, to the lord treasurer indicates that
the thefts of vagabonds and rogues are increasing and that
many escape punishment because no evidence is brought
against them. These are some of his statistics: "In all, executed this year, 1596, forty. So it appeareth, that besides
those that be executed, and those that be burnt in the hand,
35. Whipped for felony, 37. Felonies acquitted by the grand
jury, 67. Felonies acquitted by the petty jury, 45. That be
cast men, and reprieved to the gaol, there are set at liberty
this year of men committed, or bound over for felonies, 183.
The greatest part whereof must of necessity live by spoil." [6]
In that same year the Justices of the Peace of Middlesex are
asked to suppress disorderly houses in the suburbs of London
because of the "great abuses that grow by the multitude of
base tenements and houses of unlawfull and disorderly resort,"
abuses caused by "a great nomber of dissolute, loose and inso-
lent people harboured and maintained in such and like noysom
and disorderly howses, as namely poor cottages and habita-
cions of beggars and people without trade, stables, ins, ale-
howses, tavernes, garden howses converted to dwellings, ordi-
naries, dicyng howses, bowling allies and brothell howses. The
most part of which pestering those parts of the citty with disorder and uncleannes are either apt to breed contagion and
sicknes, or otherwize serve for the resort and refuge of masterles men and other idle and evill dispozed persons, and are
the cause of cozenages, thefts, and other dishonest conversa-
cion and may also be used to cover dangerous practises." [7]
To the Elizabethan these "abuses" were very real and part
of their everyday lives. They had grown up with the beggar
and his plea for alms, with the cutpurse and his dexterous
fingers. The tavern and the brothel were within walking dis-
tance. The bawds and prostitutes were carted along the

streets. Thomas Platter, visiting England in 1599, says: "I have never seen more taverns and ale-houses in my whole life than in London." [8] Platter again, on prostitutes: ". . . although close watch is kept on them, great swarms of these women haunt the town in the taverns and playhouses." [9] Platter, visiting Tyburn: "Rarely does a law day in London in all the four sessions pass without some twenty to thirty persons—both men and women—being gibbetted." [10] Eighteen years later, another traveler, Fynes Moryson, states: "Theeves in England are more common then in any other place, so farre as I have observed or heard." [11] The comments of Platter and Moryson are impressionistic, to be sure, but they reinforce what was obviously a pressing concern of the government. R. H. Tawney asserts that the sixteenth century lived "in terror of the tramp," [12] a statement that must be accepted in the light of the official documents. William Harrison, in his *Description of England,* estimates that there are more than 10,000 beggars in England,[13] and that 300 or 400 rogues are yearly hung.[14] Even these figures are topped by some calculations that over 800 persons were annually hung by the end of the century,[15] and that 80,000 vagrants sponged on the community by the 1640's.[16] The exact figures cannot be known, but all indications point to the underworld as a great and admitted social menace.

The underworld was so constant a threat that the punishment of its members was severe, by modern standards. Depending upon the number of times a vagrant was caught, he was whipped, his ear was slit or bored through with a hot iron, or he was hanged. The thief was invariably hanged, except for the most minor offenses. The Middlesex County Records, in its bare statement of punishments for offenses, makes clear the official Elizabethan attitude toward crime:

2 February, 12 Elizabeth—True Bill that . . . William Tylynge
late of London gardener stole six parcel-gilt silver spooins,
worth fifty-four shillings, of the goods and chattels of John
Tasker of London yoman. Putting himself "Guilty," William
Tylynge was sentenced to be hung.[17]

17 March, 15 Elizabeth—True Bill that, at Highholborne co.
Midd. and elsewhere in the same county on the same day,
Nocholas Welshe, Anthony Musgrove, Hugh Morice, John
Thomas, Philip Thomas, Alice Morice and Katherine Hevans,
being over fourteen years of age, and strong and fit for labour,
were masterless vagrants without any lawful means of subsis-
tence. Whereupon it was decreed that each of the said vagrants
should be whipt severely and burnt on the right ear.[18]

4 May, 14 Elizabeth—True Bill that, at Hackney on the said
day, Richard Neyler, late of London fishmonger, stole certain
hairs worth three pence from the tail of Henry Warley's mare,
and certain hairs worth three pence from the tail of John Finkes
gelding. Putting himself "Guilty," Richard Neyler was sentenced to stand in the pillory at Cheapside.[19]

The last offense vividly indicates the severity of the law in
Elizabeth's reign, a severity made necessary by a critical social
condition.

However, for many reasons,[20] vagrants continued to roam
the kingdom, thieves continued to steal. That the underworld
was more than the "fringe" of society is made clear when one
looks at Statute 14 Elizabeth (1571-2) to see what individuals
the government considered to be vagrants:

. . . all and every suche persone and persones that be or utter
themselves to be Proctours or procuratours, goinge in or about
any Countrey or Countreys within this Realme, without suffi-
cyent aucthoritye deryved from or under our Soveraigne Ladye

the Queene, and all other ydle persones goinge about in any
Countrey of the said Realme, using subtyll craftye or unlawfull
Games or Playes, and some of them fayninge themselves to have
knowledge in Phisnomye Palmestrye or other abused Scyences,
whereby they Beare the people in Hand they can tell their
Destinyes Deathes and Fortunes, and such other lyke fantasticall
Imaginacions; And all and everye persone and persones whole
and mightye in Body and able to labour, having not Lord or
Maister, nor using any lawfull Marchaundize Crafter or Mys-
terye whereby hee or shee might get his or her Lyvinge and can
gyve no reckninge how hee or shee doth lawfully get his or her
Lyvinge; and all Fencers Bearewardes Comon Players in Enter-
ludes, and Minstrels, not belonging to any Baron of this Realme
or towarde any other honorable Personage of Greater Degree;
all Juglers Pedlars Tynkers and Petye Chapmen, shall wander
abroade, and have not Lycense of two Justices of the Peace . . .
shalbee taken adjudged and deemed Roges Vacaboundes and
Sturdy Beggers, intended of by this present Act, togeather with
all and everye suche other persone and persones as shalbe here-
after for altering and breaking of such good Orders as in the
seconde part of this present Acte shalbe establyshed, for the Re-
leef of the aged and impotent poore people set forth and de-
clared to bee Vacaboundes.[21]

The persons mentioned in this statute were considered to
be rogues, vagabonds, and sturdy beggars. Add to these the
pickpocket, swindler, whore, highwayman—and one can understand, if not believe, the claim of some Elizabethans that
the underworld made up one-half of Elizabethan society. One
must allow, however, not only for exaggeration but for the
natural desire of men, especially writers, to reveal and record
the sensational rather than the humdrum. In any case, the
underworld was a social evil which not only frightened but
also interested every Elizabethan. The large amount of rogue
literature clearly demonstrates this.

The special lure that the underworld had for the Elizabethan reader is evidenced by a whole literature of pamphlets dealing with rogues, vagabonds, and cony-catchers. The first work which indicates a full interest in the subject of the underworld in England is Robert Copland's *The hye way to the Spyttel hous* (1536?) which treats of the various beggars who come to St. Bartolomew's Hospital. In 1552 appeared the first exposition of the art of cony-catching as it was practiced in the second half of the sixteenth century—*A Manifest Detection of the most vile and detestable use of Dice-play* by Gilbert Walker (?). A. V. Judges believes that this pamphlet presents "a genuine picture of the London cony-catcher who preyed upon the upper classes of society" and that it is "obviously founded on personal knowledge." [22] The next important pamphlets were John Awdeley's *The Fraternitye of Vacabondes* (1561), a listing of vagabonds and their activities, and in 1567 Thomas Harman's *A Caveat or Warening for Commen Cursetors.* Harman elaborately describes twenty-three varieties of rogues. He shows that the rogues had an organization, that they had a special language, their own traditions and ceremonies, their own hierarchy. They were, in fact, a veritable *world* within the structure of society, insulated from the outside world by their way of life and organization and speech and laws, while at the same time vitally connected to the outside world as parasite is to victim.

The writer who gave the greatest stimulus to rogue literature was Robert Greene. His pamphlets were bought and imitated throughout the rest of the century and into the next century. His followers, especially Dekker, found in Greene and in the low life of London a sure-fire topic of public interest. The rogue pamphlets became, as Louis B. Wright asserts, one of the "staple items of middle-class literary consumption." [23]

One can gain an insight into the Elizabethan attitude toward the underworld by closely investigating the rogue literature which not only provided Elizabethans with information
but reflected the readers' values, for the hack writer usually
gives the reader exactly what he wants and exactly what he
agrees with.

The rogue pamphlets were written, according to their
writers, in order to expose the activities of the underworld.
Harman feels compelled to acquaint his readers with the
"abhominable, wycked, and detestable behavior of all these
rowsey, ragged rabblement of rakehelles." [24] In the "Epistle
to the Reader" in the second impression of the pamphlet he
once again asserts his purpose: "But faithfullye for the
proffyt and benyfyt of my countrey I have done it, that the
whole body of the Realm may se and understand their lewd
lyfe and pernitious practisses, that all may spedelye helpe to
amend that is amysse." [25] To cause readers to "se and understand" is the stated purpose of those writers that succeeded
Harman in his revelations about the underworld. Greene
writes to those who desire "to know the wonderful sly devices
of this hellish crew of cony-catchers." [26] "To know their qualities" is Dekker's stated reason for writing about underworld
characters in *Lanthorne and Candle-Light*. Middleton, in his
Black Book, asserts that he is dedicating himself to "discover"
and "publish" the "monsters of nature," which he considers
the members of the underworld to be. These *stated* purposes
can be multiplied. But the pamphlets do not merely detail
the activities of the underworld—if they did they would be of
more interest to the student of crime than to the student of
literature. What the writers present in the pamphlets is more
than an exposé of methods to cut a purse or catch a cony.
They present attitudes which, if properly understood, tell us
much about the Elizabethan point of view toward the under-

world. It is this point of view which pertains directly to this study, for it affects the reception by the audience of particular members of the underworld in the drama.

All writers of rogue literature believe that the underworld is a serious threat to the commonwealth. This is, in a sense, the official attitude, since the government took pains to enforce laws against underworld members who were threats to the realm. They were a social evil, and they were attacked by rogue pamphleteers for being a social evil. Small wonder, for they were a menace in both country and city. Those rogues and vagabonds who roamed the countryside—dirty, disfigured, diseased, in tattered garments—were not only a physical fright to the country dwellers. They lived on the labors of the respectable members of the community, either stealing or forcing citizens to give alms. The well-dressed city members of the underworld were pleasant to look upon or not to be observed at all (much to the discontent of their victims), but they were equally harmful to honest Englishmen. Both the country and the city members of the underworld (and those that roamed between—the highwaymen) were, to use the words of a statute, a "great annoye of the Comon Welthe." (14 Elizabeth, 1571-2) The rogue pamphleteers reflected this attitude and emphasized the underworld's harm to society. Harman believes that the benefit to society will be great when all the rogues and vagabonds will be eliminated.

Then wyll no more this rascal rabblement raunge about the countrey. Then greater reliefe may be shewed to the poverty of eche parishe. Then shall we kepe our Horses in our pastures unstolen. Then our lynnen clothes shall and may lye safelye on our hedges untouched. Then shall we not have our clothes and lynnen hoked out at our wyndowes as well by day as by night.

. . . Then shall we safely keepe our pigges and poultrey from pylfring. Then shall we surely passe by the hygh waies leading to markets and fayres unharmed. Then shall our Shopes and bothes be unpycked and spoyled. Then shall these uncomly companies be dispersed and set to labour for their lyvinge, or hastely hang for their demerites.[27]

Greene calls the underworld a "disease," and considers its members "Machiavellians." He must expose cony-catchers, he says, because they prey upon honest citizens and seek domestic spoil and ruin. Dekker refers to the underworld as "these Rebels to the Weale-publick." "More dangerous they are to a State, then a Civill Warre, because their villanies are more subtle and more enduring" [28] In all his pamphlets he reiterates his and his reader's belief that the members of the underworld are "professed foes to the Republic," that they are "Wilde and Barbarous Rebels . . . in open armes against the Tranquility of the Weale publique." Middleton will "strip their villainies naked, and bare the infectious bulks of craft, cozenage, and panderism, the three bloodhounds of the commonwealth." [29] To Rowlands there are no more "noysome beasts in a Commonwealth" than members of the underworld;[30] they are "The Citties vermin, worse then Rats and Mice." [31] Each of these writers is disturbed about the great harm that is done to England by an element in society that lives on the sweat of others, that spreads fear and disorder. The underworld is recognized, therefore, as a social and, in many ways, a political threat, for not only did its members prey upon honest citizens but also they spread dissatisfaction with social and political conditions. Some members of the underworld were disabled soldiers turned adrift; some were victims of rent-raisings, enclosures, and evictions. These became homeless vagabonds who, rather than beg tamely, spread discontent and were potential rebels against the state. For this reason the Privy Council devoted much time and energy to enforcing the poor laws between 1530 and 1600. The underworld, in short, was attacked by government and rogue pamphleteer primarily because it was a threat to the realm.

Another major attack against the underworld rested on moral grounds. This is especially interesting to students of literature because it has repercussions in the drama. The rogue pamphleteers either blatantly professed a moral purpose in writing their tracts, or they larded their works with attacks on the immorality of some members of the underworld, or they complained of the moral damage done to England because of the presence of an underworld. Some combined this three-barrelled attack.

Thomas Harman considers the members of the underworld "abhominable" and wicked. He divulges their secrets, he maintains, in order to diminish the amount of roguery in the realm *and* to save their souls. Their souls are sinful, of course, and Harman uses every opportunity to present invective against their lewd lives.

Greene's first cony-catching pamphlet, *A Notable Discovery of Cozenage,* displays a highly moral tone. It is difficult to judge sincerity in hack work, but one feels that Greene does have a genuine desire to free himself from his evil past—at least, in this one pamphlet. "My younger years and uncertain thoughts, but now my ripe days calls on to repentant deeds, and I sorrow as much to see others wilful, as I delighted once to be wanton." To show his remorse he will discover the wiles of the cony-catchers. He does so with directness and little embellishment. Success, however, diminishes his moral fervor. In his next four pamphlets he progressively moves away from the presentation of direct information for the sake of cleansing

England to a presentation of picaresque narrative for its own sake. His last, *Black Book's Messenger,* tells of the antics of Ned Browne, "one of the most notable cutpurses, cross-biters, and cony-catchers, that ever lived in England." But even in this pamphlet some of Greene's moral fervor seeps through. Ned Browne, although he dies repentant, cannot rest in peace because of his past sins. After he is buried wolves dig him up and devour his body just as he, during his life, "delighted in rapine and stealth."

Dekker's professions of moral purpose are more prevalent and more sincere than Greene's. At every opportunity he emphasizes the bestial qualities of the underworld characters in his pamphlets. They are "savages"; their only cure is the gallows. To Dekker "ugly they are in shape and divelish in conditions"; they are "the Devils owne kindred"; their "best trades are taught in hell." [32] The relationship between the two underworlds, the Elizabethan underworld and hell, is always present in Dekker's mind. Dekker rarely sways from his stern morality. The idea of conversion, in which a thief repents and is forgiven, is not found in Dekker's rogue pamphlets, although the idea occurs often to Greene and to the writers of criminal biographies.

The other writers of rogue literature, although not so prolific as Greene and Dekker, also condemn the underworld on moral grounds. Nash's Pierce Penniless tells the Devil that he hopes the whores of London will be speedily carried to hell, "there to keepe open house for all yonge devills that come, and not let our ayre bee contaminated with theyr six penny damnation any longer." [33] The idea of contamination is a pregnant one for the rogue pamphleteers in their moral condemnation of the underworld. Samuel Rowlands expresses this idea fully in this paragraph of his *Martin Mark-All:*

For I thinke there be none here but such as you call Maunders, Clapperdugeons, and a few Padders, and those of the meanest sort, al which I may rightly term you, and give you this one name drowsie Drones, and lowsie Loyterers: and what is a Loyterer or Drone, nothing but a sucker of honie, a spoyler of corne, a destroyer of fruit, a waster of mony, a spoyler of victuall, a sucker of blood, a breaker of good orders, a seeker of brawls, a queller of life, a Baseliske of a comon-wealth, which by companie and fight doth poyson a whole countrey; and stayneth honest minds with the infection of his venome, and so draweth the Commonwealth to death and destruction, and such is the end of your lives and commanding: when we see a great number of flies in a yeere, we judg it like to be a great plague: and having so great a swarming of loytering vagabonds, and sturdie Rogues readie to brawle and swagger at every mans dore, doth it not declare a greater infection readie to ensue.[34]

Middleton attacks the members of the underworld as "speckled lumps of poison." England, for all of these writers, must be cleansed of a moral disease.

The many Elizabethans who read rogue literature were undoubtedly influenced by these attacks against the underworld on social, moral and, because of the allusions to the devil and hell, religious grounds. Rogue literature is the most obvious place to look for attitudes toward the underworld, but it is not the only place. All distributors of popular ideas played upon the underworld as a theme. The attacks against the underworld found in pamphlets other than rogue, in sermons, and in ballads are, except for degree, similar to those found in rogue literature.

Since the demand for literature of low life was great, it is not surprising to find the market invaded by hack writers with an ability to shark up quickly prose or "poetic" narratives on the lives of criminals. Gamaliel Ratsey, the thief, was

the subject of two tracts of this kind, both perhaps by the
same author. The tracts are conventional—an account of the
deeds of the criminal, followed by a confession and repentance
by the criminal himself. Just as the rogue pamphleteers attacked the underworld on social grounds, so too does the
Ratsey author. This time, however, the attack often issues
from the mouth of the thief himself. To other thieves Ratsey
seems to shout: "Villainies avaunt! you bastards are by
kinde/ That doe perturbe the countries quiet state." [35] Ratsey
feels that the thieves continuously trouble the "countries
peace." The security of the commonwealth is important—
even for the man who neglected England's laws. Ratsey also
displays a moral fervor in his repentance. Once again he chastises the thief: "God made thee man, make not thy selfe a
beast/ But seeke to love thy God with soule and strength."
The last two lines of the *Life* also shows his concern for his
soul: "And when from earth I shall dissolve to dust,/Graunt
that my soule may live among the just." An interesting wish,
especially from a man close to the brink of hell because he is
an "offender." "God is just in punishing offenders," says the
Ratsey author. The idea of God's justice is presented again
in *Ratseis Ghost:*

But the heavens are doomers of mens deedes, and God holds
a ballance in his fist, to reward with favor and to revenge with
Justice. . . . for as folly perswaded Ratsey to leade a sinfull life,
soe Justice at length brought him to a sorrowfull end, and as his
faults were fond, so his successe was foule. The wrongs he had
done cride for revenge, and pleaded to God to quitte him
with punishment.[36]

The conventional criminal biography is indeed conventional
in its attacks on the underworld.

So too is the criminal ballad, which also reveals some
underworld activities and then proceeds to a confession and
lamentation. John Clavell, in the verse tract *A Recantation of
an ill led Life,* acknowledges and confesses his offenses to
"both God and man," and then discusses the highway law.
He, like Ratsey, tells his fellow thieves: ". . . your consciences
are grosse,/ You value gaine, and not the poore mans losse."
Thieves, he says, strive against "Countrey, Justice, Law." He
realizes also his deviation from God's will, having been persuaded to sin by "The Prince of darknesse Satan, that old
theefe." (The devil-underworld association is ever present.)
Another thief, Luke Hutton, supposedly writing a ballad
the day before his hanging at York for his robberies, also
realizes he offended "my Country, and my good Queen," and
he too hopes that his sinful soul will be received by "Lord
Jesus," the "sweet Saviour." All of the criminal ballads follow
the same formula of presentation and all attack the underworld, in a sense from within, on social and moral grounds.

Sermon and homily also helped to form and disseminate
an attitude toward the underworld, although the sermons
usually did not attack specific members of the underworld.
The sermons dealt with aspects of sinful living, not very often
with members of a sinful group. The preacher would talk
against gluttony and drunkenness and whoredom and strife.
He would exhort men to obedience, to good works, to prayer.
Each weekly sermon touched on some aspect of bad living—
and bad living was exemplified by the underworld. To the
preachers drunkards, "these beastly belly-gods," are hurtful
not only to themselves but also to the commonwealth, "by
their example." "Every one that meeteth them is troubled
with brawling and contentious language, and oft-times raging
in beastly lusts, like high-fed horses, they neigh on their neighbors wives. . . . Their example is evil to them among whom

they dwell. . . . They are unprofitable to the Commonwealth. For a drunkard is neither fit to rule, nor to be ruled." [37] "An Homily against Disobedience and Wilful Rebellion" states that "thefts, robberies, and murders" are sins "most loathed of most men," although rebellion, the main subject of the homily, is the worst sin. The souls of rebels, if they repent not, are hurried into hell—the fate of all that spread mischief in the commonwealth. A rebel is, of course, the arch underworld character, because he is the cause of many robberies and murders.

> For he that nameth Rebellion, nameth not a singular or one only sin, as is Theft, Robbery, Murder, and such like; but he nameth the whole Puddle and Sink of all sins against God and man, against his Prince, his Country, his Country-men, his Parents, his Children, his Kinfolks, his Friends, and against all men universally; all sins I say, against God and all Men heaped together, nameth he that nameth Rebellion. [38]

This is the official attitude of the church toward the most infamous of criminals. Between the rebel and the drunkard can be found the whole gamut of underworld characters, all attacked by the Church (usually in connection with attributes) because they sin against countrymen and God.

A wealth of contemporary comment emphasizes that the underworld was a social and moral menace to Elizabethan society. It was a world under constant attack by preachers, ballad-makers, all kinds of pamphleteers, and the government. However, the image of the underworld that one gets from these critics is not the only image. The underworld, like Janus, had two faces—one face was feared and hated, the other was admired. Only by understanding the nature of this admiration can one have a full impression of the climate of opinion surrounding the underworld.

That some members of the underworld were admired as well as feared is the reason for the existence of so much Elizabethan rogue literature. The Elizabethans delighted in the antics of the underworld. In their daily lives the Elizabethans took pleasure in the minstrels, bearwards, pedlers, and other entertaining riffraff—all of whom were considered by law to be underworld characters. The suppression of these by Statute 14 Elizabeth, a law passed in 1572, caused much dispute between the Lords and the Commons, so that a compromise had to be reached, allowing these people to wander and perform if they had licenses. These underworld entertainers, as E. M. Leonard states, "took the place which shops, circuses and newspapers occupy in the life of today." [39] They helped to make England "merry."

In their reading the Elizabethans enjoyed accounts of men who lived by their wits. The pickpockets are the heroes of some of the best rogue pamphlets. Greene introduces his "A Tale of a Nip" with these words: "I will tell you, Gentlemen, a pleasant tale of a most singular, experienced, and approved nip . . . so well instructed . . . in his mystery that he could as well skill of a cuttlebung as a barber of a razor, and, being of a prompt wit, knew his places, persons, and circumstances, as if he had been a moral philosopher." Greene allows such complimentary phrases to dot all of his pamphlets. He praises the pickpocket because he is expert in his vocation and because he has a "prompt wit," qualities which earn him comparison with a moral philosopher in his knowledge of the way of the world—an interesting paradox in the light of the criticism of the underworld by the professional moralists. The subtitle to Greene's *Second Part of Conny-Catching* reads: "Discoursing strange cunning in Cosenage, which if you reade without laughing, I'll give you my cap for a noble." Cosenage can be a laughing matter, at least to the reader if not to the cony caught. Greene will tell "a merry tale," he says, "how a miller had his purse cut in Newgate Market." Greene can see the charm as well as the harm of the underworld. Judging from the popularity of his pamphlets, the readers evidently also saw the charm. So, too, Samuel Rid who, although exposing and criticizing those who indulge in the art of legerdemain, exclaims: "I must needs say that some deserve commendation for the nimbleness and agility of their hands." [40] Dekker, who always presents invective against the underworld and has a genuine hatred for criminals, allows a complimentary phrase to enter into his *Belman of London*. Discussing the various laws of thievery, he states: "All the former laws were attained by wit, but the *High Law* stands both upon *Wit and Manhood*." Indeed, the highwayman is the most revered member of the underworld, especially because of the two qualities mentioned by Dekker—intelligence and courage. Highway robbery was a profession fit for a gentleman. Gamaliel Ratsey is a good example of the Robin Hood kind of highwayman in whom the public delighted. The stories surrounding Ratsey are probably fictional, although he was a real thief who even has a column in the *Dictionary of National Biography*. The author or authors of the Ratsey pamphlets indicate the reason for his popularity and charm: "For hee had an eagles eye to espie advauntage, so had he a lions heart to effect his purpose." Again: "Ratsey did more by prankes and sleightes than by power and strength, for his brain was never barren of some plot or other." In true Robin Hood fashion he would rob from the rich and give to the poor. The stories usually show his humanity—for example, he robs a poor man, but realizing the man's poverty gives him back the stolen money and more to buy two much-needed cows— although the real Ratsey seems to have forgotten his philanthropy at times and indulged in callous murder. The ethics surrounding the Ratsey stories are the same ethics surrounding the Robin Hood adventures. However, Ratsey, like all offenders against God and the commonwealth, must be hanged. The Elizabethans were able to enjoy his amusing exploits, but they realized that highway robbery was a hanging matter. They did not consider Ratsey a man steeped in mortal sin, but they did consider him a rogue—and a rogue caught must pay the penalty.

Although those writing about the underworld did so with an ostensibly social and moral purpose, they often wrote with a raciness and a gusto which seems more like sympathy than satire. Some pamphleteers, by using the rogues' idiom—cant or pedler's French—gave the underworld a particular, perhaps fascinating, aura: the kind which a spectator senses when seeing a play acted in a language he only partially understands.

The reason for the popularity of the underworld in literature is, therefore, not difficult to discern. The Elizabethans loved to see "wit" at work; they respected courage, even in the heart of a highwayman; they revelled in sensation; they liked to read the speech of the jovial, although harmful, crew of rogues; they liked to laugh at some of the pranks of the underworld. The rogue spirit is essentially merry and rogues have always been connected in the public mind with a zest for life. Falstaff's "Banish plump Jack, and banish all the world!" often rings true.

In addition, some Elizabethans, because of the important role religion played in their lives, may have even felt a warmth toward members of the underworld. Perhaps somewhere in the Elizabethan mind rested the realization that Christ was hanged as a thief in place of a thief, that Mary Magdalene was a prostitute, that Lazarus was a beggar, that a whore helped Joshua. This connection between the underworld and religion, between a thief and Christ, is a pregnant relationship, stated best in a small pamphlet by a Parson Haben or Hyberdyne in which the Parson, having been robbed by thieves, is forced by them to deliver a sermon in praise of thieves and thievery. The tone of the sermon is ironic, and he makes his point at the end of the sermon, but the association of thief and Christ lingers.

. . . for they [thieves] be of all men moste stowte and hardy, and moste withowte fear; for thevery is a thynge moste usuall emonge all men, for not only yow that be here presente, but many other in dyverse places, bothe men and wemen and chyldren, rytche and poore, are dayly of thys facultye, as the hangman of tyboorne can testyfye; and that yt is allowed of god hym selfe, as it is evydente in many storayes of [the] scriptures; for yf yow looke in the hole cowrse of the byble, yow shall fynde that theves have bene beloved of gode.[41]

He takes from the Bible his examples of those thieves loved by God. Among them are Jacob, who stole his uncle's kid and who stole the blessing from his father; the children of Israel who stole Egypt's gold and silver; and Christ who took an ass and colt that was not his. He then follows with the Christ-thief relationship:

But moste of all I marvell that men can dispyse yow theves, where as in all poyntes almoste yow by lyke unto Christe hym selfe; for Chryste had noo dwellynge place; noo more have yow. Christe wente frome towne to towne; and soo doo yow. Christe was hated of all men, savynge of his freendes; and soo are yow. Christe was laid waite upon in many places; and soo are yow. Chryste at the lengthe was sawght; and so shall yow bee. he was browght before the judges; and soo shall yow bee. he was accused; and soo shall yow bee. he was condempned; and soo shall yow bee. he was hanged; and soo shall yow bee. he wente

downe into hell; and soo shall yow dooe. mary! in this one
thynge yow dyffer frome hym, for he rose agayne and assendid
into heaven; and soo shall yow never dooe, withowte godes
great mercy, which gode grawnte yow! to whome with the
father, and the soone, and the hooly ghoste, bee all honore and
glorye for ever and ever. Amen![42]

The Parson makes his point well, and stops the thief-Christ association in the best place—in hell, where all rogues and
thieves congregate. However, the thieves liked the Parson's
sermon so much that they gave him back his money and
two shillings for the sermon.

Some members of the underworld were, if not admired,
at least accepted as part of a general, and natural, scheme
of life based on competition, thievery, and cheating. Not that
public morality was necessarily low—there are no valid statistics with which to test it, and opinions about morality
usually come from those contemporary commentators who
tend to look for the worst. The reflections of the "water
poet," John Taylor, are interesting in this connection. His
verse displays a constant search for clever comparisons and
ideas, but in his own way he presents what could be considered common attitudes toward the underworld. After
describing Mercury as the god of thieves, he says:

> Thus Thieving is not altogether Base
> But is descended from a lofty Race.
> Moreover every man, himselfe doth showe
> To be the Sonne of Addam, for we knowe
> He stole the Fruite, and ever since his Seede,
> To steale from one another have agreede.[43]

This assertion that thieving is, in a sense, natural leads to
a description of thieving by all members of society. When

Taylor comes to the "real" thieves, those who are legitimately members of the underworld, he shows that they are in some respects beneficial to society—they create labor.

> And sure I thinke, that Common Burglaries,
> Pick-pockets, High-way Thieves, and Pilferies,
> And all that thus Felloniously doe Thieve,
> Are Thieves whose labours many doe Relieve,
> Who but poore Thieves doe Jaylors wants supply?
> On whom doe under Keepers still rely?
> From Thieving money still is gotten thus,
> From many a Warrant and a Mittimus,
> And if men were not apt to Filch and Thieve,
> 'Twere worse for many a High, and under-Shrieve.
> The Halter-maker, and the Smith are getters
> For Fatall Twist and pond'rous Bolts and Fetters.
> . . .
> The Ballad-maker doth some profit reape,
> And makes a Tiburne Dirge, exceeding Cheape,
> The whil'st the Printers, and the dolefull Singers,
> Doe in these gainefull business dip their fingers.
> The very Hangman hath the sleight and skill,
> To extract all his goods from others Ill,
> He is the Epilogue unto the Law,
> And from the jawes of Death his life doth draw.[44]

Just as he finds that everyone is a thief, so too everyone is a bawd. His poem, *A Bawd,* bears out his statement that "All Bawdry doth not breed below the middle." [45] Many ideas found in Taylor's poetry are playful, to be sure, but they coincide with similar ideas expressed by other writers. One finds, for example, this sentiment in Carlos Garcia's *The Sonne of the Rogue,* Englished by W. M. in 1638: "For if it be true that we are all partakers of Adams sinne, his sin being nothing else but to robbe God of his knowledge, it is evident, that there is in us an inclination, disposition and naturall desire to robbe and steale." [46] Because, as Garcia asserts, thievery can be considered a "naturall desire," practised by all members of society, the attitude toward the particular member of the underworld who steals and cheats must be softened. This is most clearly expressed in a rogue pamphlet, Samuel Rowlands' *Martin Mark-All*. Corporal Fize, an underworld character, asks the Belman why he rails against "us poore Vagrants, peniless pilgrimes" and neglects those that are far more damaging to society. The comment is important enough to quote in full.

Let us poore folke live as we doe, we doe no man hurt but our selves, nor no mans foe but our owne, we have nothing but what other men can spare, other mens leavings are our refreshings, and if it were not for us, much good meate would be in danger of Fly-blowing, or cast to dogges. If there bee any in our vocation or calling, that live disorderly and out of compasse, what trade can you name that doe not the like. If wee sometimes lie with our neighbors wives, is it not usuall else-where? . . . If then it be all one in City as in Countrey, among the rich as amongst us poore, and generally in all Trades and Occupations deceit and abuses, sith it is so that he that cannot dissemble cannot live: why then should you bee so spitefull goodman Sounsbell to inveigh against us poore soules above the rest, who of all others, in shifting are the most simplest soules in this over wise world.

But you good sir, like a Spider to entrappe onely the smallest flies, suffer the great ones to flie through, you scowre the ditch of a company of croaking frogs, when you leave behinde you an infinite number or venemous Toades, you decypher and paint out a poore Rogue, or a Doxie that steale and rob hedges of a few ragged clothers (which you can make but petit larciney.) And never speake of those Vultures that ruine whole Lordships, and infect the commonwealth, by their villainous living to the discredit of some, and ill example of all.[47]

Here is an underworld character criticizing other worlds and interests that are infectious to the commonwealth. Rowlands, specifically attacking the underworld in this pamphlet, presents a wider criticism of the age by having the underworld attack other "caterpillars in the commonwealth."

Whereas the official literature, statute and sermon, emphasized the underworld's threat to man and God, the rogue literature, also stressing the threat, played upon the sensational and amusing aspects of crime, and even presented conycatching as a symbol of general economic cheating. The Elizabethan attitude toward the underworld seems to be composed, therefore, of a series of contradictions. The members of the underworld were feared as social and political dangers to the realm; they were chastised because of their sinful natures; they were the Devil's advocates and they belonged in hell. At the same time some were praised for their wit and courage, laughed at for their antics, and associated with Christ. The Elizabethans were able to enjoy the exploits of the underworld, in print if not in reality, and also to enjoy the underworld's punishment. By presenting a dual image to the Elizabethan mind, the underworld was able, by its very nature, to serve as a richly ambivalent element in Elizabethan drama, evoking in the audience a dual awareness. How the particular dramatist used the image is the subject of this study. The climate of opinion surrounding the underworld provides a useful frame of reference for observing a dramatist's mind and art. It is not the only frame of reference, for the underworld was also part of a specific dramatic tradition.

2

The Morality Tradition

Dramatic treatment of the underworld begins with the morality plays. However, glimpses of this world can be found in the miracle plays. Only glimpses, to be sure, because the subject matter of the miracles was predetermined. Most medieval dramatists rarely strayed from their particular Biblical sources. They wished to present to their audiences important stories of the Bible; their aim was religious. Some dramatists, however, did allow the life around them to find its way into their Bible stories, and with this life came the representation, here and there, of an underworld.

It is a critical cliché that as drama progressed in England from its beginning to its flourishing in the Elizabethan age it came closer and closer to the real life of the streets. It is, therefore, best at the outset to speculate why the medieval dramatist, when he brought the life around him into his

play, often chose the underworld; why, in fact, an examina-
tion of the use of the underworld in miracle and morality
play clearly indicates the drift of the drama toward realism.
The most obvious, and most important, reason for its entrance
into medieval drama is that the underworld can become, with
little or no effort by the dramatist, part of the moral pattern
of a play. It is not only a world of evil, but a world of *present*
evil, immediately felt as compared to an abstract idea of evil
(and, even more so, as opposed to an abstract idea of good.)
It was a world that was there, all around the playgoer, and
with its built-in moral shading it was a convenient part of
society for the dramatist to exploit. In short, the underworld
provided immediacy or contemporaneity *and* could easily be
used to make a moral point. In addition, since it typified a
seamy side of life that was coarse, boisterous, and merry, it
could be used as an effective vehicle for amusement. And the
underworld's evocation of the double attitude, as demonstrated in Chapter 1, allowed the playgoer to enjoy playing
the Devil's advocate for a short while, thereby fulfilling a
human need. The specific function of the underworld in a
particular play is, of course, determined by the play; but whatever the function, the emergence of realism and the use of the
underworld are directly related.

In the miracle plays, various characters are called thieves
and beggars; one finds much talk about hanging; the relationship between thief and hell is often present. The references
to the underworld come easily to the mouths of the actors.
That God tells Cain in the Chester *Creation* that he will be
"Idle and waved like a theefe," that a mother in the York
Massacre of the Innocents calls the soldiers who are seizing
infants "theves," that Herod calls the three wise men "land
lepars" (vagabonds) in the Towneley *Herod the Great,* are
what one would perhaps expect in the particular contexts.

The underworld, in these allusions, is not developed in action. References to the underworld do, however, enter the action in the plays dealing with the crucifixion of Christ. It is with these references that a discussion of the underworld in English drama must begin.

Christ was crucified as a thief, in place of a thief, and with a thief on each side of him. It is this Biblical fact that allows the anonymous writers of miracle plays to use the underworld as material for drama. The Chester cycle makes the most vivid use of the Christ-thief relationship. Annas, one of the villains of Christ's Passion, shouts:

> bring forth those theves two!
> on eyther syde of him shall they goe,
> this Sir shall be honored so
> with fellowship in feere.
>
> (425-428)

The fellowship between this Sir, Christ, and the two thieves is the central human element in the play. Almost 300 lines after Annas' command, as the three thieves hang—a representation intrinsically charged with emotion—the first thief taunts Christ, saying that Christ should save them if he really *is* God's son. The second thief urges the first not to make "thy frend thy foe." He then says:

> Man, thou knows well, iwysse,
> that righteously we suffer this,
> but this man hath not done amis,
> to suffer so great annoye.
> But, lord, I beseech thee,
> when thou art in majesty,
> then that thou wilt thinke on me,
> And on me have mercy.
>
> (713-720)

Christ promises the second thief that he will join him in paradise. Only the Gospel according to St. Luke (**XXIII,** 39-43)
contains an account of the first thief's taunting and the second
thief's answer. The Chester playwright recognized its dramatic interest and incorporated it in his play. The next play of
the cycle, *Christ's Descent into Hell,* where the fulfillment of
Christ's prophecy is witnessed, goes beyond the Biblical account. The second thief appears, bearing a cross on his shoul-
ders, and speaks to Adam. He is saved because he realized
that Jesus was God's son. That he enters bearing the cross
is a fine dramatic touch—it vividly symbolizes not only the
torment of the thief, but also the thief's closeness to Christ.
His appearance demonstrates that Christ's promise was kept.
The dramatist's aim was religious, and his method was vividly
dramatic.

The scene is interesting in yet another respect. The ambiguity in the climate of moral opinion surrounding the underworld is built into the story of Christ and the two thieves.
That a man is a thief need not necessarily condemn him in
the eyes of the audience, for it does not condemn him in the
eyes of Jesus. The same is true for a whore, as the Mary
Magdalene story clearly demonstrates. The underworld can
sometimes be on the side of God. Yet the underworld remains
a world of evil, for even Jesus is indignant that the soldiers in
the York play *The Agony and The Betrayal* seize him "like
a theffe heneusly," and in a later play Mary mourns that her
son "Hyngis as a theffe." When this ambiguity, simple here,
becomes more complex and interesting in the plays of later
writers, the underworld will become a rich dramatic world.

The writers of miracle plays did not often go beyond their
sources. When they did they invariably touched upon the life
around them, usually the seamy side of life. The very play
that contained the thief bearing the cross, the Chester *Christ's*

Descent, depicts a scene in hell, where an alewife appears to
Satan and his demons. Woeful to be in hell, she tells of her
cheating in the tavern, specifically pointing out that she
watered the brew and kept no true measure. She asserts that
she will inform against the tapsters of the city who, breaking
the "statutes of this cuntrey,/hurtinge the common welth,"
will land, as she did, in hell. The Chester dramatist, fully
exploiting the contemporary alewife, presents nothing less than
a low-life scene in a Biblical play, and manages to carry on a
rogue-pamphlet crusade, with the alewife exposing the cheating
of tapsters because they harm the commonwealth. A. C.
Cawley, asserting that "the final scene of the offending alewife, funny though it is, has nothing whatever to do with the
rest of the pageant," [1] dismisses the scene too lightly, for it
does have a connection with the main story. Satan says that
although Jesus has gone away with the people who have occupied Hell, the alewife can abide there. Hell will be occupied
again by the kind of person the alewife typifies. The Chester
alewife is the first in a parade of cheaters, thieves, whores, and
murderers who will occupy hell.

The denunciation of tapsters and the fact that they are hell-
bound is also found in the Chester *Slaying of the Innocents.*
A demon, sent by Lucifer to take Herod to hell, utters the
following lines, which are extraneous to the subject-matter of
the play:

> No more shall you, Tapstars, by my lewty,
> that fills ther measures falcly,
> shall bear this lord Company;
> The gett none other grace.
>
> I will bring this into woe,
> and come agayne and fetch moe,
> as fast as ever I may goe.

(449-455)

The writer, who seems compelled to mention the antics of the tapsters as an abuse of his time, perhaps wished to show his audience that hell is here, now, and that it is ready to receive all those who cheat their neighbors. This kind of jump from Herod of the Bible going to hell to the tapster in the nearby tavern going to hell sows the seeds of a purely secular drama. The life around the writers of miracle plays managed to push its way into their Biblical accounts.

This tendency toward realism is evident in the Towneley mysteries, where devils are merry and coarse, where Noah's wife is shrewish, where Cain is a vulgar rustic. It is a thief, however, who provides the Towneley writer with his most vital element of realism. The dramatist's use of Mak's exploits as sheep-stealer in *The Second Shepherds' Play* is important to this study because it clearly looks ahead to the use of the underworld in the moralities and in Elizabethan drama. The introduction of Mak, with his southern accent and thieving ways, gives the Christmas scenes an immediacy which the dramatist obviously intended. Mak's stealing of the sheep and hiding it in the cradle is "an astonishing parody of the Nativity itself," [2] a "mock-nativity." [3] Mak's scenes in the play, therefore, not only contribute to the general Christmas mirth, but produce vivid associations with the Christ story. In the Chester plays, Christ redeems a thief. In *The Second Shepherds' Play* a thief puts a stolen sheep in a cradle; the association between sheep and cradle points directly to that very Christ the Redeemer. It is too serious a notion to consider Mak "the comic antithesis to Christ" and to relate him to the legend of the Antichrist.[4] Mak is a thief, and indeed a thief's way of life is anti-Christian, but his function in the play is primarily to provide mirth. His punishment, being tossed in a blanket, is appropriate to the play's tone, but is not the "realistic" punishment of a thief. Mak the thief is, in a sense, redeemed by the Christmas atmosphere of joy, by the Christ who has just been born. A thief in a miracle play, therefore, has provided immediacy and mirth, and his antics have reflected upon the main action of the play. This will be the exact function of many members of the underworld in later drama.

The drift toward realism is also clearly illustrated in the Digby *Conversion of St. Paul.* Saul asks for a horse in order that he may go out and punish Christian rebels. His servant and an ostler—the scene undoubtedly shifting to an inn—then have an exchange of words, filled with language relating to cow turd and horse dung. The exchange is there for the sake of comedy alone; the scene is incidental. The inn, however, has entered a miracle play; contemporary life, in a setting, has been crudely pulled into Biblical story.

The tavern has an important dramatic function in the Digby *Mary Magdalene,* a play which contains elements from both miracle and morality play. The Digby dramatist presents all of the conventional features of the Biblical Mary Magdalene story, but he includes the struggle of good and bad forces for the soul of Mary. In a scene that takes place in hell, Satan opens a debate on Mary Magdalene. If she remains virtuous, she will destroy hell, Satan declares. Therefore, Lechery must seduce her, and the other evil spirits will help bring her to hell. In the next scene Lechery, a woman, flatters Mary—a Satanic device—and advises her to amuse herself. Since the tavern is the best place for amusement, Lechery leads Mary there. In the tavern scene the Taverner tells the two women that he is the best taverner in Jerusalem and that he sells all kinds of wine. Lechery orders the best wine. Then a gallant enters, called Coryoste; he is a dandy who has "new com to town." He wants to chat with "sum praty tasppyster." Lechery tells Mary "this man is for yow." The Magdalene readily agrees. Coryoste makes love to Mary,

who declares that she likes him. In the course of their conversation she coyly asks him: "wene ye that I were a kelle?"
(Do you think I'm a prostitute?) They leave together. It
is in the next scene that the Bad Angel informs the audience
that Mary granted all that Coryoste wished for—indeed, she
becomes a "kelle." She has reached the lower moral depths;
the Devil can rejoice. Three scenes later, however, she laments
her sin, and resolves to seek Christ. From this point on the
story is conventional; the Bible takes over.

Mary Magdalene (c.1480-1520) is important to this study
because it contains the first tavern scene *on stage;* it is the
first in a long line of such scenes pointing toward the Boar's
Head Tavern. Here one finds a whore, a gallant, a taverner,
an evil tempter. The Digby dramatist wanted his audience to
witness the sin of Mary Magdalene, and so he leads her to a
tavern, the logical place for sin. It becomes the stereotyped
place for sin in the moralities. E. K. Chambers believes that
with this play "we have to do less with a mystery beginning
to show morality elements than with a deliberate combination
effected by a writer familiar with both forms of drama." [5]
The Digby dramatist was not an innovator. Realistic elements
entered the miracle plays before he wrote his play. The tavern material is part of a trend toward realism best exemplified
by the Towneley mysteries. But until more evidence is found
to the contrary, it can at least be said that with the dramatized
tavern scene the Digby dramatist presents, for the first time,
a basic ingredient of the morality plays in a miracle play.

The morality play is a dramatized allegory. It is based on
the conflict between Good and Evil for the soul of Man, a
conflict basic to Christianity. It is homiletic in purpose and
method. Whether the morality play is an early one or a late
one, the conflict remains essentially the same—only the
names are changed. This being the only prerequisite for all

writers of moralities, they had a freer hand with their choice
of material than did the writers of miracle plays. The general
scheme of all morality plays is this—Man, first good, is corrupted by a Vice figure, who causes Man to sin, and then
Man, now bad, becomes converted to good again.[6] Within
this scheme much ingenuity is possible. Eventually, the generalized humanity of the moralities became so human, so
particularized, that the time was ready for a Shakespeare.
The underworld played an important part in this development.

Perhaps it is inherently human for man to find Evil more
enjoyable and more interesting than Good. Certainly the
writers of morality plays presented the forces of evil with a
zest and vividness never achieved by the forces of good.
The writers were on the side of the angels, but they toyed
with the Devil—as did Man in his pilgrimage through a world
of sin. Because the underworld was by its very nature an
evil world, and because it was a world in the closest contact
with the dramatist's audience, it was the most natural source
for the dramatist's world of sin. Some of the early moralities,
written before 1500, already demonstrate this clearly.

Mind, Will, and Understanding (1450-1500)[7] is a highly
serious play in which Mind, Will, and Understanding are
corrupted by Lucifer, and eventually saved by Wisdom. The
dramatist confines himself to the allegorical world of the play.
Once, however, he alludes to the world outside. Will particu-
larly favors the opposite sex; he considers woman "a hewynly
syght," although heaven is far from his thoughts when he
says this. While he is in a state of corruption he asserts that
he prospers in London and "to the stews I resort." This
statement, in fact, helps to *indicate* his corruption. The stews
of London, and its inhabitants, are evil. They help the writer
to produce an immoral atmosphere around a specific charac-

ter. This becomes one of the underworld's most important
functions.

What is an allusion in *Mind, Will, and Understanding*
becomes an important plot element in *Mankind* (1450-1500).
The framework of this morality is conventional—Mankind,
at first a follower of Mercy, is tempted by the forces of evil,
falls, and is finally saved. But the action is often farcical, and
the dialogue is often obscene. Baugh believes that "as a
morality play it is so debased as to be rather a contradiction
of the type." [8] This is too harsh. Willard Farnham is on
safer ground when he asserts that in *Mankind* "the broad
humor is more generously admixed than in any previous morality," but that "the central other-worldly teaching is still
secure: man fell originally through disobedience; now in his
baseness of inherited evil he must turn to the mercy of God
for redemption." [9] The underworld is part of this "inherited
evil."

The forces of evil that seduce Mankind are Mischief, at-
tended by the three devils, Newguise, Nowadays, and Nought,
and Titivillus. When Nought appears he introduces himself
with these words:

> My name ys "Nought"; I love well to make mery;
> I have be sethen with ye comyn tapster of Bury;
> I pleyde so longe the foll, that I am ewyn wery wery;
> Yyt xall I be ther ageyn to-morrow.

(266-269)

That he was with the tapster of Bury and that he loves to
make merry informs the audience of his character. He and
his cohorts fail in their initial attempt to divert Mankind,
who calls them "thevys." However, Titivillus, shrewder than
the rest, does succeed. He tells Mankind that Mercy, Man-

kind's guide, has been hanged for stealing a horse. Mankind
immediately becomes happy, and declares that he will go
to the alehouse and get a wench.

> Whope! who! Mercy hath brokyn hys nekekycher a-vows;
> Or he hangyth by the neke hye upp on the gallouse.
> A-dew, fayer mastere! I wyll hast me to the alehouse,
> Ande speke with New-gyse, Now-a-days & Nought,
> A(nd) geett me a lemman with a smattrynge face
>   (600-604)

The immediacy of his reaction is not surprising, because one
finds little soul-searching in morality plays. But the nature of
his reaction does indicate his corruption. His willlingness to
go to a tavern and meet a "lemman" is the dramatist's way
of showing the beginning of Mankind's temporary pilgrimage to hell. Under the influence of the vice characters, he
is ready to become an underworld character. He obediently
answers "I wyll, ser" to the orders of Mischief, who himself
is presented as a member of the underworld, for he earlier
informed the audience that he was chained, that he killed his
jailer, kissed the jailor's widow, and stole some goods. Mankind agrees to kill, steal, and rob, to give up church services,
and to wear a dagger to cut people's throats. The last is expressed in this way:

MYSCHEFF: Ye must have be yowur syde a longe "de pacem,"
           As trew men ryde be the wey, for to on-brace them;
           Take ther money, kytt ther throtes! thus over-face
               them:
           "I wyll," sey ye!
MANKYNDE: I wyll, ser.

                                                   (707-710)

With this "I wyll" Mankind reaches an ethical low. From

here he must rise, as he does, and is finally won over by
Mercy.

The *Mankind* playwright makes good use of the underworld. He alludes to the perennial tapster to indicate the
character of Nought, presents Mischief as a murderer and
thief, has Mercy falsely accused of being a thief, causes Mankind to be overjoyed with the thoughts of a wench in a
tavern, and shows Mankind's willingness to be a highwayman. The underworld is the world of evil that Mankind
embraces before he can be pulled loose by Mercy.

The atmosphere of the New Learning pervades Henry Medwall's *Nature* (1490-1501). The morality framework is evident, but the force of good is Reason, opposed to the evil
Sensuality. The goal, therefore, is less a heavenly kingdom
than a rational life here on earth. The play is filled with references to the life of London, of which the underworld references are by far the most important. During the Life-in-
Sin phase of the play Sensuality suggests to Man: "Hardly
let us two go/ To some tavern here beside." Man willingly
goes. The audience does not see him in the tavern, but learns
about his activities from Sensuality's report to Pride and
Worldly Affection:

> By my faith! we sat together
> At the tavern, next hereby;
> And, anon, who should come together
> But flee(r)ing Kate and Margery.
>   . . .
> Marry! Reason, that ye two spake of
> Came even to us as we say so drinking;
> And gave our master a heat, worth a hanging,
> Because that Margery sat on his knee,
> While that other whore sat talking with me.
>   (p.78, 79)

Sensuality sums it all up with: "He is now as familiar/
With bodily lust as ever ye were." At the end of Part I
Man goes back to Reason, but in Part II he admits that
since he "did to Reason assent/ I had never a merry day."
Sensuality tells Man that Margery will be glad that he has
returned to his old ways. He emphasizes her sadness:

> And, because she would live in penance
> Her sorrow for to quench,
> She hath entered into a religious place,
> At the Green Friars hereby.
>
> (p.92)

Evidently, Margery has gotten herself to a nunnery! Sensuality and Man then have an interesting conversation concerning this "religious place." Man asks if the women there are
"close nuns as others be."

SENS.: Ye must beware of that gere!
        Nay, all is open that they do there;
        As open as a goose eye!
MAN: And cometh any man into their cells?
SENS.: Yea, yea, God forbid else!
        It is free for everybody;
            . . .
MAN: Be they not wedded, as other folk be?
SENS.: Wedded, quod a? no, so mot I thee!
        They will not tarry therefore;
        They can wed themselves alone.
        "Come kiss me, John;" "Gramercy, Joan!"
        Thus wed they evermore.
                                              (p.92)

Bodily Lust then tries to persuade Man to go to a brothel.
Man is on the horns of a dilemma—should he go to the

particular whore Margery or to a brothel? The dilemma itself indicates how low he has come. Bodily Lust leaves to
see how things are at the brothel, only to return and report
that the brothel whore is busy with a nobleman: "Hence,
Forty Pence! quo' she, Jack Noble is a-bed!/ This night ye
come too late." So Man goes to Margery. Man undoubtedly
did not miss his chance to visit the brothel afterward, because
Pride mentions that he must look for Man there. When
Man gets old, he repents and is forgiven by Reason.

Because Sensuality is the main opponent of Reason, Medwall concentrates on the tavern and brothel aspects of the
underworld. Man's sinfulness is most effectively presented by
his association with whores. His immoral dilemma—whether
to choose a tavern whore or a brothel whore—accentuates
his wantonness; at this point in the play there seems little
hope for his salvation. But mercy prevails, with the help, one
cannot help feeling, of an old age that dries up the juices
of sensuality.

John Rastell's *The Nature of the Four Elements* (1517-18)
is, in many respects, similar to Medwall's *Nature*. Small wonder, for as Bernard Spivack asserts, "Both men belonged to
the intellectual and literary circle that seems to have had its
center in the household of Cardinal Morton and contained as
well the young Thomas More. Medwall was Morton's chap-
lain and Rastell became More's brother-in-law, and there can
be little doubt of their personal acquaintance, or of Rastell's
knowledge of Medwall's plays." [10] Rastell presents a representation of mankind, here called Humanity, who instead of
following Studious Desire is seduced by Sensual Appetite. In
Four Elements, as in *Nature,* the energetic low-life of London
plays an important role. Before Humanity is won back by
Natura naturata—which the reader can assume even though
the last pages of the play are imperfect—he must pass through

the tavern world and romp with the whores. When Humanity says that he is hungry, Sensual Appetite immediately
suggests going to a tavern. The Taverner enters and talks
about his different wines, a la *Mary Magdalene*. When
Sensual asks the Taverner if he can get Humanity "any good
meat?" and when Humanity says he would like "a good
stewed capon," the Taverner says:

> Though all capons be gone, what then?
> Yet I can get you a stewed hen,
> That is ready dight.
> HUM.:   If she be fat, it will do well.
> TAV.:   Fat or lean, I cannot tell,
> But as for this I wot well
> She lay at the stews all night.
>
> (p.20)

The Bankside brothels must enter, even in a play on words.
Sensual describes to Humanity the pleasures of the tavern,
where he will find little Nell, Jane, and Bouncing Bess. Humanity does go to the offstage tavern, where he undoubtedly
had a merry time, for, as he admits to Sensual, the company
at the tavern was "mich merrier" than the company of Studious Desire. So, Sensual suggests that they go back to the
tavern, where Humanity can satisfy his "wanton lust." Once
again the London underworld of tavern and brothel is used
to designate the waywardness of man. In this play, with its
emphasis on the new values of the Renaissance, its function
is to take Humanity away from an intellectual contemplation
of the world.

About five years after the presentation of *Four Elements,
Mundus et Infans* (1500-22) is printed, a play which takes
its delinquent hero from Infancy to Old Age. Therefore, it,
like *Mankind,* is concerned with the moral problems connected

with life in general, not with any specific Renaissance problem. Yet, the vehicle by which the dramatist presents his hero at his lowest moral level remains the London underworld. Manhode is not only fascinated by the sinful world of taverns and stews, but is eventually clapped into Newgate prison. He is very interested in the adventures of Folye. It is in the following description by Folye that the dramatist becomes most specific about the life around him; he seems compelled to localize the world of the play in order to make it vivid for his audience.

> By my feyth, syr, into London I ran
> To the tavernes to drynke the wyne;
> And than to the innes I toke the waye,
> And there I was not welcome to the osteler,
> But I was welcome to the fayre tapester,
> And to all the housholde I was ryght dere,
> For I have dwelled with her many a daye.
> . . .
> I feythe, syr, over London-brydge I ran,
> And the streyght waye to the stewes I came,
> And toke lodgynge for a nyght;
> And there I founde my brother, Lechery:
> There men and women dyde folye,
> And every man made of me as worthy
> As thoughe I hadde ben a knyght.
>
> (584-590; 592-598)

The London tavern and stews are brought in not only for the sake of realism, but also to indicate the character of one of man's enemies. Manhode, when he is old and broken and called Age, laments that he did not listen to Conscience and keep Christ's commandments. Because he followed Folye he was "set in stockes" and in Newgate he "laye under lockes." All ends well for him, however, because he repents his folly and turns to God.

The drift toward realism becomes more pronounced as the sixteenth century progresses,[11] causing a change in the shape of the moral drama. The representative of generalized humanity becomes more individualized; the forces of evil lose some of their abstract qualities. The plays themselves change in purpose—the dramatized allegory shifts its emphasis from the allegory to the drama. The process involved in all of this is not a sequential one; the changes in a play in one year do not lead to the changes in a play the following year. By looking at the whole body of morality plays presented in the sixteenth century, especially at the underworld elements in these plays, the trend is discernible.

Hyckescorner (1513-16) reveals some of this change in the drama. Its cast contains six characters: Hyckescorner, Imagynacyon, Frewyll, Pyte, Contemplacyon, Perserveraunce— the first three bad, the last three good. The names suggest a morality, but there is no real struggle for Mankind. The scene is the London of the audience. When Frewyll enters, he introduces himself; for the audience to know his character he immediately and conventionally refers to the stews: "But at the stewes syde I lost a grote." When Imagynacyon enters, he complains of "a payre of sore buttockes" because he was clasped in a pair of stocks. Imagynacyon tells Frewyll about Hyckescorner, pointing out that they dwelled together at Newgate; he also refers to Tyburn. He boasts that he "can stele with my tethe," "can loke in a mannes face and pycke his purse." Then Hyckescorner appears. Imagynacyon is surprised to see him: "Hyt was tolde me that ye were hanged." Hyckescorner reveals that his friends are "theves and hores" and "other good company," who have "made a-vowe forever to dwell in Englonde." The three characters, obviously

recognizable by now as members of the underworld, discuss
their plans for the evening:

> At the stues we wyll to-night.
>
> . . .
>
> Let us kepe company all togyder,
> And I wolde that we had Goddes curse
> If we some-where do not get a purse!
>
> Every man bere his dagger naked in his honde,
> And, if we mete a treue man, make him stonde,
>   Or elles that he bere a strype!
> If that he struggle and make ony werke,
> Lyghtly stryke hym to the herte,
>   And throwe hym into Temmes quyte!
>
>   (406; 411-419)

The three decide to accuse Pyte of theft and put him in the
stocks, thereby giving him the punishment that they deserve.
Pyte resigns himself to his fate; he is Christ-like in his having
to suffer like a thief. He then laments the corruption of the
age:

> Youth walketh by nyght with swerdes and knyves,
> And, ever amonge, true men leseth theyr lyvese:
> Lyke heretykes we occupy other mennes wyves
>   Now-a-dayes in Englonde.
> Baudes be the dystryers of many yonge women,
> And full lewde counseyll they gyve unto them.
>
> . . .
>
> Courtyers go gaye and take lytell wages,
> And many with harlottes at the taverne hauntes.
>
>   (561-566;584,5)

Frewyll enters to tell where he has been—where one would
expect: at the tavern, drinking and stealing. When Per-

severaunce and Contemplacyon want to sway him from sin, he shouts at them:

> Avaunt, catyfe! dost thou thou me?
> I am come of good kynne, I tell the:
> My moder was a lady of the stewes blode born,
> And, knyght of the halter, my fader ware an horne.
>
> (703-706)

Being an underworld character is a family tradition for him, and he is proud of it. When Imagynacyon enters again he boasts that he was made a "knyght of the coller" at Tyburn, and that he is now also controller of the stews. Perseveraunce tells Imagynacyon that God hanged on a tree and lost His blood for him, to which Imagynacyon replies:

> What devyll, what is that to me?
> By Goddes fast, I was ten yere in Newgate,
> And many more felawes with me sate,
> Yet he never came there to helpe me ne my company.
>
> (946-949)

But Imagynacyon and Frewyll do repent. Nothing is heard or seen of Hyckescorner.

The realism in this play is directly associated with the underworld. The three personifications of evil are its members. Through them contemporary London breaks into the play, the London of Newgate, Tyburn, and the stews. Such a London must be corrected; therefore, the playwright, through the words of Pyte, reveals the corruption of the age. Although Frewyll and Imagynacyon repent, Hyckescorner still roams the streets of London. It is Hyckescorner, interestingly enough, who gives the play its name.

The generic figure of Mankind becomes narrowed to the

generic figure of Youth in the play called *Youth* (1513-29).
The dramatist is concerned with the problem of contemporary
youth; therefore, he uses contemporary London as a setting
and the London underworld as a moral force. The plot is
simple and conventional: Youth, who enters as a profligate,
does not heed Charity's advice for good living; he is a companion of Riot, the play's vice character, who is helped by
Pride and Lechery in the seduction of Youth; in the end
Youth repents.

Youth comes on stage already filled with vices. He boasts
about his own body, and is very insulting to the religious
Charity, with whom he offers to fight, but then says:

> No, sir, I think ye will not fight;
> But to take a man's purse in the night
> Ye will not say nay;
> For such holy caitiffs
> Were wont to be thieves,
> And such would be hanged as high
> As a man may see with his eye.
>
> (p.97)

That Youth considers the good Charity to be an underworld
member reflects on his own character. Riot *is* a member of
the underworld, as the following conversation makes clear:

YOUTH: What, I weened thou hadst been hanged,
          But I see thou art escaped,
          For it was told me here
          You took a man on the ear,
          That his purse in your bosom did fly,
          And so in Newgate you did lie.
RIOT: Verily, sir, the rope brake,
          And so I fell to the ground,
          And ran away, safe and sound:

By the way I met with a courtier's lad,
And twenty nobles of gold in his purse he had:
I took the lad on the ear,
Beside his horse I felled him there:
I took his purse in my hand,
And twenty nobles therein I fand.
Lord, how I was merry!

(p.99)

Riot suggests to Youth that they go to the ever-present tavern, where they can drink and where Youth shall have "a wench to kiss." Later, Lechery—the name suggests a personification but her actions suggest a fleshy whore—dallies with Youth. Toward the end of the play, when Charity insists that Youth mend his ways "That thou may'st save that God hath bought," Youth says:

What say ye, Master Charity?
What hath God bought for me?
By my troth, I know not
Whether that he goeth in white or black;
He came never at the stews,
Nor in no place, where I do use.

(p.113)

The suggestion of meeting Christ at the stews may have been shocking to the audience and probably casts the darkest reflection on Youth's character, but immediately afterward he repents, unconvincingly. The tavern, the stews, Newgate, hanging, purse-stealing—all help to give the play a sense of realism and to indicate the depths that profligate youth can reach.

The problem of youth is also treated in *The Nice Wanton* (1547-53), a more realistic play than *Youth*. Only two characters retain their allegorical names, Worldly Shame and Iniquity. The former has the function of a chorus in only one scene; the latter is allegorical in name only. According to Thomas Marc Parrott, *The Nice Wanton* is "a primitive form of Domestic Tragedy." [12] Such a label in itself indicates that the morality play is beginning to deal with the particular immediate problems of the bourgeoisie, in this case with the bringing up of children.

Xantippe has three children: Barnabas, Ismael, and Dalilah. She did not spare the rod on the former, but spoiled the latter two. Consequently, Barnabas is good, and Ismael and Dalilah are bad. Eulalia, a friend, complains to Xantippe about her children: "Your sonne is suspect lyght-fyngered to be;/ Your daughter hath nyce trickes three or foure." She tells her not to spare the rod, but Xantippe tells Eulalia to mind her own business. When Ismael and Dalilah are first seen, they are casting dice with a gallant, Iniquity. Iniquity refers to Ismael's "lyght-fyngered" quality: "I must have some of the mony/ Thou hast pickt out of thy fathers purse." Ismael loses, but says he will get more money: "By Gogs, bloud, I wyll robbe the next I mete!/ Yea, and it be my father." Judging from the dialogue, one can assume he *prefers* to rob his father. When Ismael leaves, Iniquity and Dalilah discuss what they have won. It seems that they, like true rogues, worked together to cozen Ismael. Also like true rogues, they fight over the money. When Dalilah leaves, Iniquity exclaims: "Thief brother, syster whore,/ Two gragges of an yll tree!" After a long interval, according to the stage directions, Ismael is accused by Judge Daniel of "felony, burglary and murdre." After the verdict comes in that he is guilty, the judge declares that he will be hanged. Iniquity, in an attempt to bribe the judge, is also sentenced to death as an accomplice of Ismael. Worldly Shame then reports that Dalilah, now a whore at the stews, "is dead of the pockes," and that Ismael is hanged. Worldly Shame tells Xantippe:

"Every man saith thy daughter was a strong whore,/ And thy sonne a strong thief and a murderer, to." Xantippe is stopped from killing herself by her son Barnabas, who states that his brother and sister at least repented before they died.

The problem of Youth, therefore, has become the problem of particular youths in a family situation. The moral teaching in a struggle of Good against Evil becomes a presentation of the truth of a maxim: Spare the rod and spoil the child. Youth, who associated with members of the underworld, has become Ismael and Dalilah, who *are* members of the underworld. The dramatist, in teaching his lesson, places the two spoiled children in what he undoubtedly considers to be the worst situation. Significantly, the boy becomes a thief and murderer, the girl a professional whore. They die the deaths of such underworld characters, by hanging and by the pox. The underworld gives the realism of the play its very essence, and the dramatist uses this realism to strengthen his moral lesson.

The upbringing of youth is the subject of other plays in the morality tradition. Three of these—*The Longer Thou Livest, the More Fool Thou Art* (1559-68), *Misogonus* (1560-77), and *The Marriage between Wit and Wisdom* (c. 1579)— once again display the underworld as an important element in the drama's drift toward realism.

As a youth, Moros, the hero of *Longer Thou Livest,* is incorrigible. He defeats all the efforts of his parents to give him the proper education and piety. He would much rather enjoy the company of his friends Idleness, Incontinence, and Wrath. Therefore, his time is spent in drinking, gambling, and wenching. His evil friends become his teachers:

> We will teache thee to play at cardes and dice,
> Aqueinted with Nell and Nan we will thee make.

. . .

> We meane to eate, drinke, and make good cheere,
> With Pegge and Besse to be ruffeling.
>
> (D1ᵛ)

They teach Moros well, as is evident when Incontinence reports his activities:

> It is a world to see the fooles greedines,
> I have nuseled him incarnalitye,
> A man would marvell to see his redines,
> Unto all fleshly sensualitie,
> And these harlots are not to learne,
> How to dally with a simple foole,
> They may leade him with a thred of yearne,
> Into the middest of a whyrle poole.
>
> (D4)

His sinfulness as a youth affects his life as a man. Nothing excitingly new is happening here: a representation of Youth is led to wenching by vice characters, and the wenching helps to signify his depravity.

Misogonus is another matter. It is a racy play, in which the underworld is presented vividly. Misogonus is the product of poor upbringing; he is another spoiled child who becomes addicted to drinking and wenching. Philogonus is in despair because his son seems irredeemable.

> A company of knaves he hath also on his hand
> Which leads him to all manner lewdness apace;
> With harlots and varlets and bauds he is manned;
> To the gallows, I fear me, he is tradding the trace.
>
> (p. 141)

The tavern scene vigorously portrays Misogonus and some other profligates, among whom are Melissa, the whore, and the licentious priest Sir John. The scene is filled with drinking, dicing, and dancing. The relationship between Misogonus and Melissa—"She's none of these coy dames, She's as good as Brown Bessie"—points up his sinfulness. The dramatist has brought the tavern world with all its activities on stage. In doing so, he has presented one of the liveliest pieces of realism in the morality tradition, a realism which makes stronger the moral lesson.

Whereas the realism of the tavern scene in *Misogonus* has a dramatic purpose, the realism in *The Marriage between Wit and Wisdom* is usually there for its own sake. In it the underworld runs rampant. The plot concerns the attempt of Young Wit, a product of a mixed upbringing by his father Severity and his mother Indulgence, to win Lady Wisdom. He is sidetracked, however, by Idleness, the Vice, who provides the play with its low comedy and who is, in many respects, an underworld character. Wit tells Idleness he is looking for some pleasant pastime, to which Idleness replies: "I am even as fit for that purpose as a rope for a thief." A playful underworld allusion from a personification who *is* a thief. As one would expect, Idleness' female companion is a whore, called Wantonness. Wantonness is big with child. Idleness, trying to mate Wantonness and Wit, tells her:

> Nay, but in any wise hide your belly.
> WANT.: It is a child of your getting.
> IDLE.: I, it hath fathers at large:
> But here comes in Wit that is like to bear all the charge.

> (p. 268)

Wantonness lulls Wit to sleep on her lap. Idleness then steals Wit's purse away. He tells the audience: "my fingers

are as good as a lime twig." He then utters the dictum of
thievery:

> The bee have no so many herbs whereout to suck honey,
> As I can find shifts whereby to get money.

Two soldiers then enter, singing that they "live by spoil":

> Now we are come from Flusing to the English port,
> There shall not a fat pouch
> Come nodding by the way
> But Snatch and Catch will desire him to stay.
>
> (p. 273)

Like so many soldiers in the rogue pamphlets, Snatch and
Catch (their names indicate their activities) are members of
the underworld. They take away from Idleness the purse
he stole from Wit. Idleness puts on a number of disguises
in order to escape the law for his stealing of Wit's purse. His
last disguise is that of a beggar. He utters the plea of many
a rogue-pamphlet beggar:

> Give me one penny or a halfpenny,
> For a poor man that hath had great loss by sea,
> And is in great misery.
> God save my good master, and my good dame,
> And all the householder!
> I pray you bestow your alms of a poor man
> Nigh starved with cold.
> Now I am a bold beggar—I tell you, the stoutest of my kin,
> For if nobody will come out, I will be so bold to go in!
>
> (p. 289)

He goes in and steals a pot, a common beggarly practice.
Inquisition catches him and takes him to prison. He will

"be whipped up and down the town next market day." In his parting address to the audience, Idleness points out that he will continue to "play the purveyor here on earth for the devil." All of the antics of Idleness are presented for the sake of entertainment. His underworld characteristics—his purse stealing, his association with the whore, his disguise and theft as a beggar, his being an agent of the Devil—have little bearing on the plot of the play. The dramatist is interested in the underworld purely as material for comedy. The sheer force of the underworld's image as a world of merriment pulls this morality play very close to realistic comedy. Bits of realism for comic purposes and for providing a sense of immediacy have entered the drama from its beginning, but here in *Wit and Wisdom* realism pervades a string of episodes that comprise what could be considered an inconsequential sub-plot, thereby indicating the potential use of the underworld as a structural element in later drama. The underworld could serve not only as an important part of the main plot of a play, but could at times comprise, as it does in *Wit and Wisdom,* a sub-plot presented for comic appeal alone.

Another play, not concerned with youth, which vividly shows the close contact between the subject matter of a morality and the subject matter of realistic comedy is Ulpian Fulwell's *Like Will to Like* (1562-68). Here Mankind has become six typical characters from real life who represent evil living. Because the Vice, Nichol Newfangle, brings each of these characters to his proper fate, the audience is given clear evidence that good living leads to happiness and evil living leads to punishment and hell. The play's didactic purpose is emphasized in the prologue:

> Herein, as it were in a glass, see you may,
> The advancement of virtue, of vice the decay.
>
> (p. 4)

However, Fulwell becomes too engrossed in the glass's reflection of vice; it is with the humorous scenes of London low-life that the play becomes alive.

Of the representatives of evil, the two that directly pertain to this study are Cuthbert Cutpurse and Pierce Pickpurse. The stage direction describes their entrance: "Cuthbert Cutpurse must have in his hand a purse with money or counters in it, and a knife in one hand and a whetstone in the other; and Pierce must have money or counters in his hand and jingle it, as he cometh in." Both immediately describe their activities:

CUTH: By Gog's wounds, it doth me good to the heart,
     To see how cleanly I played this part.
     While they stood thrusting together in the throng,
     I began to go them among;
     And with this knife, which here you do see,
     I cut away this purse cleanly.
PIER: And also, so soon as I had espied
     A woman in the throng, whose purse was fat,
     I took it by the strings, and cleanly it untied:
     She knew no more of it than Gib our cat.
                      (p. 28)

They are overjoyed to see Nichol Newfangle, an old friend. Nichol reminds them of their ancestry:

For thou, Cuthbert Cutpurse, was Cuthbert Cutthroat's son
And thou, Pierce Pickpurse, by that time thou hast done,
Canst derive thy pedigree from an ancient house:
Thy father was Tom Thief, and thy mother was Tib Louise.
                      (p. 29)

This kind of inbreeding was commonly reported in rogue literature. The three leave the stage singing a drinking song.

The next time the two thieves appear they have halters
around their necks, because Nichol has betrayed them to
Severity, the judge. Cuthbert curses Nichol, laments the "hour
wherein I was born," and says that he should be a mirror to
all to "flee from evil company." Pierce says: "Let us call
to God for his mercy and grace." Hankin Hangman enters;
Nichol addresses him:

> Come, Hankin Hangman, let us two cast lots,
> And between us divide a couple of coats:
> Take thou the one, and the other shall be mine.
> Come, Hankin Hangman, thou cam'st in good time.
>
> (p. 50)

They take off the coats of Cuthbert and Pierce, and divide
them—a parody of the casting of lots for Christ's coat. This
parody works in behalf of the thieves, for their association
with Christ, added to their conventional rogue-pamphlet repentance, evokes in the audience the dual awareness that is
part of the climate of opinion surrounding the underworld.
Fulwell's purpose—to show the results of evil living—is not
effectively served by having the audience sympathize even
vaguely with Cuthbert and Pierce, who are led out by
Hankin, presumably to their deaths. His moral lesson is
somewhat weakened by the force of the conventional image of
the underworld, but this does not detract from the underworld's function as a source of realism and comedy. Fulwell
is obviously concerned with the vices of his time, and his
desire to correct them is genuine enough. But the play must
have been enjoyed primarily for its humorous low-life scenes.
Cuthbert and Pierce, according to Willard Thorp, "boast of
their achievements like rascals stepped out from the pages of
Greene's pamphlets." [13] The comparison is a good one. Just

as Greene's rogue pamphlets were presented for correction and amusement, so too Fulwell's *Like Will to Like*. In both cases, amusement usually overshadowed correction.

Many are the plays in the sixteenth century which conform to the morality pattern, but which concern topical matters. Once Mankind is fragmented, there is no limit to the particular categories of humanity that a dramatist can use, nor is there a limit to the kind of problems he can deal with. Politics and economics can become the proper subject matter for morality-type plays, as can historical and Biblical subjects. The range is great; the only limiting factor is the ingenuity of the individual dramatist. Regardless of the play's source or interest, the underworld usually finds its way into the dialogue or action.

John Skelton's *Magnyfycence* (1515-23) is a political morality. The vices of the play—Counterfet Countenance, Crafty Conveyance, Cloaked Collusion, and Courtly Abusion—are political vices, evils prevalent at court. Yet, their qualities are universal. For example, Counterfet Countenance, appearing on stage alone, tells about himself. He asserts that he stands for falsity and deceit, and that he is relied upon by men in all walks of life, specifically mentioning thieves. Crafty Conveyance admits that he aids petty thieves in escaping detection. Folly, another representation of evil, describes the various people he makes fools of, pointing out that he causes idle men to commit robbery:

> Syr, of my maner I shall tell you the playne:
> Fyrst I lay before them by bybyll
> And teche them howe they sholde syt ydyll
> To pyke theyr fyngers all the day longe;
> So in theyr eyre I synge them a songe
> And make them so longe to muse

That some of them renneth strayght to the stuse;
To thefte and bryboury I make some fall,
And pyke a locke and clyme a wall.

                    (1220-1228)

Toward the end of the play, Counterfet, Crafty, and Cloaked
Collusion dispute about which is the cleverer thief; they refer
to the opening of locks, the opening of chests containing valu-
ables, the stealing of wallets. After mocking Magnyfycence
they decide to go the places where most morality vices and
victims go:

          And to the taverne let us drawe nere.
          And from thens to the halfe strete,
          To get us there some freshe mete.
          (2262-2264)

The "halfe strete" is on the Bankside, where the stews are
located.

The underworld references in Skelton's play have no deep
significance; they do, however, help him to accentuate the
evil qualities of his vice characters. Although the vices are
directly involved with politics, Skelton's subject, they refer,
in the course of the play, to more common matters of everyday experience—the picking of locks, the stealing of wallets,
the stews, the tavern. The underworld, in short, helps to
reveal that the qualities of the vices are universal.

John Bale, in his strongly political anti-papal *King John*
(1530-36), needs no assistance from the underworld in attacking Rome. However, an interesting reference does enter
the dialogue. Sedition, now that King John has been under-
mined, exults that "Our Holy Father (the Pope) maye now
lyve at hys pleasure,/ And have habundaunce of wenches,
wynes, and treasure." Now that the Protestant king is over-

thrown, the Pope can, at least figuratively, visit the tavern world—where fallen Mankind always goes.

In the political drama *Albion, Knight* (1537-66), Division, explaining to Injury how he will divide the state, points out that he will spread the rumor that Principality does not protect the commonwealth: "But thieves and raveners, and murderers eke,/ Daily true men they pursue and seek." The underworld is here, as it is in the rogue pamphlets, a symptom of the disorder in the commonwealth. So too in *Wealth and Health* (1553-57), where the vices, Ill Will and Shrewd Wit, do their best to thwart both Wealth and Health, and thereby injure the economics welfare of the state. Shrewd Wit's song indicates his character:

> I come now out of a place
> Where is a company of small grace
> Theves and whores that spendes a pace
> They were dronken all the sorte.
> One of their purses I did aspy
> Out of his sleve where it dyd lye
> And one wynked on me with his eye
> But there began the sporte.
>   Their false falsehode, and I crafty wyt
> got the purse loe, heare I have it
> I ran my way and let hym syt
> Smoke and shitten arse together.
>   (349-360)

He and Ill Will are, as Remedy recognizes, "false theves"—obvious enemies of the state in a play based on economic issues.

The corruption of the law through bribery is the specific object of attack in Thomas Lupton's *All for Money* (1559-77). The play consists of one basic situation: many petitioners, representing various social types, appear before All-for-Money, either a "ruler or magistrate," to plead their cases. They are ushered in to see All-for-Money by Sinne, the Vice, who boasts of his attributes in this way:

> No picking of purses can be at market or fayer,
> No theft or robberie, no murther or killing
> Can be without me, ne yet whordome or swearing.
> (B2ᵛ)

Among the petitioners are two underworld characters, Gregory Graceless and Moneyless-and-Friendless. Gregory, "that can cut a mans purse and looke in his face," tells All-for-Money his plight:

> Mine neighbors saye they will hang me because I am a theefe.
> The last night I chaunced to take a budget with two hundred
> pound,
> And maymed also the partie that they thinke he will die,
> The budget with money I did hyde in the ground:
> So that they mist it although they tooke me,
> Therefore for your ayde to you nowe I flie:
> And the one halfe shall you have for saving my life,
> And the other must keepe my house, my children and my wife.
> (D1)

He succeeds in escaping punishment. Immediately after him appears Moneyless-and-Friendless to tell his story:

> O my Lord, as I came by an hedge the last night,
> Of a fewe ragges and clothes I chanst to have a sight:
> Which when I had vewed with me I them tooke,
> Which were not worth a crowne I dare sweare on a booke:
> And I have a riche neighbour that threates me verie sore,
> That I shalbe hanged right shortly therefore.
> (D1ᵛ)

In a play based on the bribery of the law, the presentation
of underworld characters is not unusual. Here Lupton presents the highest and lowest kinds of thief, the highwayman
and the beggar who robs clothes from hedges. Each is a
typical member of the underworld in a play which is essentially a satirical comedy of manners. The morality tradition
seems to be stretching its bounds.

Liberality and Prodigality (1567-8) also concerns Money
and also contains the underworld. In the play the writer
dramatizes the experiences of Money in the hands of Prodigality, Tenacity, and Liberality. The lesson he wishes to teach
is a worldly one: prudence in handling money—a far cry
from the spiritual purposes of the early moralities. Money,
because he has been ill-treated by Prodigality and his bosom
companions, Tom Tosse and Dick Dicer (who are first seen
in front of a tavern talking to Dandelyne, the tavern hostess),
decides to leave them and go to Tenacity. When Prodigality,
Tom and Dick learn this they become desperate—Money is
important to them—and plan a robbery. They not only
rob Money but they also kill Tenacity. They are now full-
fledged members of the underworld. In a later scene a
Constable appears, making hue and cry. He is searching for
the three robbers and murderers. Then the Sheriff reports that
Prodigality has been caught. A realistic courtroom scene
follows. The clerk reads the indictment to Prodigality:

Thou art indited here by the name of Prodigality, for that thou
. . . together with two other malefactors yet unknowne, . . .
didst felloniously take from Tenacity . . . one thousand pounds of
gold and silver starling: And also, how thy selfe, the said
Prodigalitie, with a sword, price twenty shilling, then and there
cruelly didst give the saide Tenacitie upon the head, one mortall
wound, whereof hee is now dead, contrarie to the Queenes peace,
her Crowne and dignitie.

When he pleads guilty the judge sentences him "to be hanged till thou be dead." Prodigality repents according to the fashion of rogue-pamphlet and rogue-ballad criminals.

In describing this play Tucker Brooke asserts that "the author is continually straying from one side to the other of the line which separates symbolism and actuality, obscuring his moral by little aimless sallies into the realm of picaresque realism." [14] These little sallies, however, give the play its life. The court scene, the talking of Tom and Dick in front of the tavern, the constable's hue and cry, are injections of vital realism into a play that is dull without them. And the sallies are not altogether aimless. In addition to providing amusement, they enforce the point of the play by stressing the actual *presence* of evil. In *Liberty and Prodigality,* the morality tradition forces a personification called Prodigality to rob another personification called Money. Thirty years later, in a realistic play, another prodigal, Falstaff, will rob money.

The Bible as a source for drama did not stop with the miracle plays, although few writers of moralities saw fit to use it. Those that did were able to do so with a free hand; they invariably brought into the plays the world around them, including the underworld. The writer of *John the Evangelist* (1520-57) is interested in contrasting spiritual and earthly love. Eugenio and Actio are young men in the full swing of a pleasurable, worldly, acquisitive life on earth. Both are frequenters of taverns and lovers of evil women. St. John and Irisdision preach to them throughout the play, and convert them in the end. In the course of one of his lectures to Eugenio, Irisdision says that those "that worketh the devels wyll" go to hell. He points out that there are many paths to hell, to which Eugenio says:

> Than one can not fayle where he go by nyghte or daye
> But may a man go to the stewes that waye
> At his pleasure if he lyst to playe.
>
> (130-132)

Eugenio likes to think that the path to hell is the primrose path of dalliance. The play's Vice, Evil Counsel, is also a frequenter of the stews. When asked by Irisdision where he lives, Evil Counsel says: "Syr at the stewes is my most abydynge." No better place for a Vice to live and for a youth to visit in that part of his life which is sinful.

In *Godly Queen Hester* (1525-29) the three vices—Pride, Adulation, and Ambition—complain that Haman, the play's villain, has cornered the market on all of their qualities; they decide to go to "the tavern door." Their function in the play is not at all dramatic; they merely point up Haman's all-embracing wickedness. But they cannot leave the stage without the tavern allusion. The tavern is the proper place for the vices, even when they can only drown their sorrows.

Mary Magdalene, the subject of a miracle play verging on the morality, is also the subject of a full-fledged morality by Lewis Wager—*The Life and Repentaunce of Marie Magdalene* (1550-66). Wager is a strong Protestant who attempts to dramatize the sinfulness of a wanton life and who, at the same time, wishes to present a model of repentance. It is in the wanton part of Mary's life that the play has its greatest vitality and its greatest realism. The vices teach her the trade of a whore, emphasizing clothes and cosmetics, but the blushes on her cheeks reveal her true character, which comes to light only after Christ enters the play. Once she is an experienced sinner, the Vice, Infidelity, acts as her pander and gives her some consoling advice:

In good faith when ye are come to be an old maude,
Then it will be best for you to play the baude.
In our countrey there be suche olde mother bees,
Which are glad to cloke baudry for their fees.
This is the order, such as were harlots in their youth
May use to be baudes, evermore, for a truth.

(700-705)

There is nothing in this play to compare with the tavern scene in the Digby *Mary Magdalene,* but in his sensitive presentation of Mary Magdalene as a sinner, Wager brings a character in a morality play to the brink of the morality tradition. Dekker's Bellafront does not seem too far in the future.

When plays conform to the requirements of the morality in some respects—usually in didactic purpose and personified abstractions—but present real characters from contemporary life or history or romance, they gather as many labels to describe their particular mixtures of genre as Polonius' listing of the players' repertoire. The labels, however, do tell a tale, for in the very mixture one finds the significant beginnings of literal drama. As the sixteenth century progresses, the drama is moving more and more in the direction of the naturalistic, and the underworld helps to push it along.

Thomas Preston's *Cambises* (1558-70) is a mixture of the morality and the historical tragedy. The story is historical, but Preston retains some abstractions. These, however, are not successfully abstract. The world around him seems to push Preston away from the morality tradition, as his presentation of the character Meretrix clearly demonstrates. Meretrix enters the play when Ambidexter, the Vice, is fighting with three ruffianly soldiers, Huf, Snuf, and Ruf. She is a whore, as her name indicates, and a camp follower; she goes where the boys are. She enters with these words: "What, is there no lads heer that hath a lust,/ To have a passing trull to help at

their need?" The soldiers are happy to see her. She, like most
Elizabethan whores, looks for gifts: "What will ye give me?"
Then she recognizes Ambidexter, who says he "must have
a kisse." She readily agrees. But one kiss is not enough for
Meretrix; she takes more. When Ruf says "Gogs heart, the
whore would not kisse me yet," Meretrix is quick to answer:
"If I be a whore, thou art a knave, then it is quit." She says
she will sleep that night "with him that giveth the most
money." Since Huf has no money, he leaves. Ruf offers six-
pence, to which Meretrix replies: "Gogs heart, slave, doost
thou think I am a sixpenny jug?" Snuff outbids his rival by
offering eighteen pence. Ruf and Snuf begin to fight, with
Meretrix joining in. Ambidexter "must run his way for
feare," according to the stage direction. Snuf then flees, and
Meretrix overpowers Ruf, who becomes her servant. They
leave the stage with her comment:

> Then let me see how before me ye can go:
> When I spake to you ye shall do so;
> Of with your cap at place and at boord:
> Forsooth, mistres *Meretrix,* at every word.
> Tut, tut; in the camp such souldiers there be;
> One good woman would beat away two or three.
> Wel, I am sure, customers tary at home:
> Manerly before; and let us be gone.

(p. 267)

This little scene indicates that the underworld has become
so common an element in the drama that it can lose its serious function and yet find its way naturally into a serious
play. One can say that Ambidexter's encounter with the
soldiers indicates that he can play upon low characters as
well as high, but the scene becomes farcical with the entrance
of Meretrix. Preston is here interested in the comedy alone,

with Meretrix used specifically for that purpose. She has the
qualities of most Elizabethan stage whores—she loves money,
she dislikes being called a whore, she aims at respectability
(Ruf must call her "mistres"), she is lustful, as her profession
demands. No moral atmosphere, however, is hovering around
her whorishness. She is a far cry from the Besses and Madges
with whom Man plays in the sinful world of the tavern and
stews. She is a lively wench who will become a Doll Tearsheet when touched by the pen of a Shakespeare. Whereas
Falstaff speaks "in King Cambises' vein," Doll Tearsheet acts
in Meretrix's vein.

Meretrix is the play's only visible member of the underworld, but another underworld character lurks among the
audience. When Ambidexter enters, he says:

> In deed, as ye say, I have been absent a long space:
> But is not my cosin *Cutpurse* with you in the mene time?
> To it, to it, *Cosin;* and do your office fine.
>
> (p. 291)

Before leaving the scene, he says:

> But how now, cousin Cutpurse? with whome play you?
> Take heed, for his hand is groping even now:
> Cosin, take heed, if ye doo secretly grope;
> If ye be taken, cosin, ye must looke through a rope.
>
> (p. 291)

And again, before the banquet of Cambises and his queen:

> He is as honest a man as ever spur'd cow;
> My cosin *Cutpurse*, I meane, I beseech ye judge you:
> Beleeve me, cosin, if to be the kings gest, ye could be taken,
> I trust, that offer would not be forsaken.
> But, cosin, because to that office ye are not like to come,

Frequent your exercises, a horne on your thumb,
A quick eye, a sharp knife, at hand a receiver:
But then take heed, cosin, ye be a clenly convayor;
Content your self, cosin, for this banquit you are unfit,
When such as I at the same am not worth to sit.

                                             (p. 306)

Ambidexter seems almost compelled to refer to his "cosin
Cutpurse." Perhaps his words are merely playful, as they are
when Haphazard, another Vice, refers to his "Cousin Cutpurse" in *Appius and Virginia* (1559-67). Then again, and
more likely, perhaps the words are not *merely* playful. The
kinship between the cutpurse and Ambidexter is a reflection
on Ambidexter's function in the play, because Ambidexter,
like the cutpurse, "with bothe hands finely can play." The
cutpurse is *dexterous,* in the most obvious way; Ambidexter
is more politic. The Vice represents a quality that is found
everywhere, affecting Cambises and the court *and* Hob and
Lob, Huf, Snuf, and Ruf. His association with a cutpurse
circulating among the audience makes his quality even more
present. Even when Ambidexter leaves the stage, what he
represents, in the person of his "cosin Cutpurse," is shifting
among the viewers of the play—a clever theatrical trick for
the often crude Thomas Preston.

Common Conditions (1576) is a mixture of morality and
romance, with the slightest emphasis on the former. The
Vice, Common Conditions, circulates in a plot filled with
every kind of romantic cliché—good knights, bad knights,
jealous ladies, dutiful ladies, pirates, robbers, exotic islands,
strange forests. The underworld is part of the conglomeration
of incidents that make up the plot. Three tinkers, Thrift,
Shift, and Drift, enter talking. In the course of their conversation, Thrift says: "By Gog's blood! let us leave off tinking,
and follow them (Sedmond and Clarisia) to purloin." Tink-

ing is not so profitable a vocation as thieving. Shift points
out that "We will take away their purses." They wait for
their victims behind a bush, and then confront Sedmond and
Clarisia, accompanied by Common Conditions. They tell
Common that they will hang him. He states that he would
rather hang himself, to which Thrift says: "By Gog's blood,
my masters! and he will we are all content;/ For then, in
time, for hanging him we need not repent." This is an interesting comment in the light of all the popular literature wherein a rogue repents in the end for his crimes; it undoubtedly
struck a responsive chord in the audience. Common tricks
them by climbing up the tree and calling for help. They
flee, and Thrift, Shift, and Drift are seen no more. The
incident has some importance in the plot because the antics of
the tinkers separate Sedmond and Clarisia, who must now
be followed separately in the plot. But the main function of
the tinker-robbers is comic diversion. In addition, these
realistic characters give the romance, as Spivack asserts, "a
fillip of vulgarity." [16] They are representatives of low life,
and their encounter with the representatives of the world of
romance gives that world its proper perspective. In a later
world of romance another representative of the underworld
will enter for the same reason; he will be called Autolycus.

The personified abstractions of the morality tradition are
part of what is essentially a comedy of manners in *The Three
Ladies of London* (1581), attributed to Robert Wilson. It
professes to be "A Perfect Patterne for All Estates to looke
into." The plot involves the wooing of the three ladies, Love,
Conscience, and Lucre, by various suitors. Fraud, who enters
"like a ruffian," states that he is going to London to serve
one of the three ladies; he cares not whom so long as he gets
"pence." Simplicity, who is present throughout the play and
is not so simple as his name suggests, recognizes Fraud for

the cozener he is. He points out that Fraud, when he worked as an ostler, doubled the bills of the guests and greased the teeth of the horses so that they should eat no hay—exactly the kind of tricks described in the rogue pamphlets. Later in the play Conscience also dwells upon the deceits of the ostler and tapster. Rather than be involved in any kind of deceit, Conscience decides to sell brooms. Simplicity would rather be a beggar:

> Faith, I'll go even a-begging: why, 'tis a good
>   trade; a man shall be sure to thrive;
> For I am sure my prayers will get bread and cheese,
>   and my singing will get me drink.
>
>   (p. 327)

The next time Simplicity appears on stage, he is a beggar in the company of two other beggars, Tom Beggar and Wily Will. They all enter singing this song:

> To the wedding, to the wedding, to the wedding go we:
> To the wedding a-begging, a-begging all three.
>
> Tom Beggar shall brave it, and Wily Will too,
> Simplicity shall knave it, wherever we go:
> With lustly bravado, take care that care will,
> To catch it and snatch it we have the brave skill.
>
> Our fingers are lime-twigs, and barbers we be,
> To catch sheets from hedges most pleasant to see:
> Then to the alewife roundly we set them to sail,
> And spend the money merrily upon her good ale.
>
>   (p. 347)

They are merry souls who love the life they lead. Tom, in fact, is very explicit about the advantages of a beggar's life:

Now, truly, my masters of all occupations under
    the sun, begging is the best;
For when a man is weary, then he may lay him down
    to rest.
Tell me, is it not a lord's life in summer to
    louse one under a hedge,
And then, leaving that game, may go clip and coll
    his Madge?
Or else may walk to take the wholesome air abroad
    for his delight,
When he may tumble on the grass, have sweet smells,
    and see many a pretty sight?
Why, an emperor for all his wealth can have but
    his pleasure,
And surely I would not lose my charter of liberty
    for all the king's treasure.

                                        (p. 347)

Wily Will will also not forego "this ancient freedom," and
he too surrounds the life of the beggar with an aura of
romanticism. Simplicity complains to his fellow beggars that
they are cozening him. When Fraud enters, and Tom and
Will act friendly toward him, Simplicity leaves. Fraud be-
littles the beggar's life, which Tom and Will had so enthusias-
tically praised:

You seem to be sound men in every joint and limb,
And can ye live in this sort to go up and down the country
    a-begging?
O base minds: I trow I had rather hack it out by the
    highway-side,
Than such misery and penury still to abide.

                                        (p. 352)

Beggary is for base fellows; it is better to be a highwayman, the king of the underworld. Fraud tells them that his lady, Lucre, wants Mercatore the merchant to be robbed, and they are the likely men to do the job. They agree, and leave the stage with Fraud, who will lead them in the theft. The robbery takes place off stage, and Simplicity is falsely accused of aiding the robbers. He enters with Serviceable Diligence, the Constable, and, as the stage direction states, "an Officer to whip him or two, if you can." After some joking with the Constable that he wishes to be whipped on the skin in order to save his clothes—a realistic touch—Simplicity is whipped on stage, and then they exit. In the play's end, Lucre is accused of robbing Mercatore and consenting to the murder of Hospitality. No mention is made of the beggars.

The play clearly demonstrates that realism is the primary interest of the dramatist, despite his personifications. He dramatizes much rogue literature and presents two flesh-and-blood characters in the persons of Tom Beggar and Wily Will. The on-stage whipping of Simplicity, the falsely accused robber, is merely a transference of a street scene to a stage scene. Such characters and incidents stretch the morality tradition to its ultimate bounds.

So too does *A Knack to Know a Knave* (1592), the last play to be considered in this chapter. This play is a blending of morality and history and comedy of manners and romance; it therefore makes a fitting conclusion to a discussion of morality compounds. The personification Honesty has a knack to know knaves. He demonstrates this knack to Saxon King Edgar by exposing the Bailiff of Hexham's four sons. One of the four sons is a Coneycatcher—one of those "caterpillars" who "corrupt the commonwealth," in King Edgar's words. The Bailiff shows the proper admiration for an underworld character when he addresses his son Coneycatcher:

And first to thee, my son, that liv'st by wit:
I know thou hast so many honest sleights,
To shift and cosen smoothly on thy wit,
To cog and lie, and brave it with the best,
That 'twere but labour lost to counsel thee.

(p. 516)

Honesty considers Coneycatcher to be "an arch cosener"; he
has watched him many times at the Exchange. The audience
is allowed to observe a scene in which Coneycatcher cozens
a broker; this is rogue material dramatized. Honesty confronts Coneycatcher with ". . . you are Cutbert the Coneycatcher,/ The bailiff's son of Hexham, whose father, being
dead,/ The devil carried to hell for his knavery." Coneycatcher tells of his own qualities, with an emphasis on wit.

'Tis strange to see how men of our knowledge live,
And how we are hated of the baser sort,
Because, forsooth, we live upon our wit:
But let the baser sort think as they will,
For he may best be termed a gentleman,
That, when all fails, can live upon his wit.
And if all fails, then have I got a wench
That cuts and deals to maintain my expense.

(p. 573)

Honesty and the king, disguised, trick Coneycatcher into be-
traying himself. The king, unable to endure the falsity of
Coneycatcher, exclaims:

Peace! shameless villain, execrable wretch,
Monster of nature, degenerate miscreant!
. . .
Have I such monstrous vipers in my land,
That with their very breaths infect the air?

(p. 542)

These are the exact sentiments of the rogue pamphleteers. Coneycatcher will be manacled and his forehead will be scarred.

An important part of the play, therefore, is essentially a rogue pamphlet on the boards. Honesty acts like Dekker's Belman of London, who also has a knack to know a knave. Coneycatcher is a typical cozener in qualities and method. The king's attitude toward him is also typical of the attitude of rogue pamphleteers and other producers of popular literature. The climate of opinion surrounding the real underworld hovers here also. With this play the circle comes full round: it uses dying morality materials to present contemporary realities; it expresses dramatically what was discussed in Chapter 1.

An investigation of the moralities from *Mankind* to *A Knack to Know a Knave* indicates that the drama was moving from the homiletic to the natural, from the abstract to the concrete, although this development was not strictly sequential. As the drama moved, so too did the underworld, often even faster than the drama itself. The personifications of evil were the most "human" personifications in the moralities. The dramatists carved their personifications of goodness and purity from heavy wood. For their representations of evil they often used flesh and blood—as if to indicate in their art that the flesh is attractive. W. Roy Mackenzie calls the vices "a troop of as virile, resourceful, red-blooded scoundrels as one could wish to meet—or avoid." [17] In an attempt to make their plays vivid and immediate, the dramatists reached into the world around them. In fact, it is more correct to say they reached into the underworld around them. They injected into their plays the taverns with their Bouncing Besses, the stews, the pickpurses, the robbers, the murderers, Newgate, Tyburn. It is natural, perhaps unavoidable, for the

abstract tavern world of a play to gather to itself the characteristics of the real tavern down the road. When this tendency
becomes compelling, when the pull of the outside world becomes too great, then the morality tradition must decay.

Decay it does, but it never dies.[18] Christopher Marlowe's
Dr. Faustus indicates both the decadence of the tradition and
the life that clings to it. Marlowe's use of the Good and
Evil Angels, the Old Man, and the Seven Deadly Sins is too
easy. It produces too obvious a symbolism and tends to over-
simplify the struggle between Hell and grace in Faustus' huge
mind and breast. But with the tavern image Marlowe demonstrates how useful and meaningful a morality element can
become. For the tavern in *Dr. Faustus* becomes the twenty-
four-year period of voluptuousness and forbidden knowledge
which Faustus experiences after his pact with the devil. Just
as Mankind, on his road to hell, visited the tavern world to
experience the pleasures of sin, so too does Faustus. He too
is "wanton and lascivious." The difference is in degree. Mankind is content with a tavern wench; Faustus must have Helen
of Troy. The tavern of *Dr. Faustus* embraces more than a
wench, a drink, or a theft. It embraces Sin, it embraces
Hell, it embraces the World—which *is* Hell. The tavern, in
the hands of Marlowe, becomes the world of Sin in all its
implications. Having experienced this world, Faustus is
doomed. Whereas Mankind received a last-minute reprieve,
Faustus sees ugly hell gaping. His fate is tragic, for he will
never see the face of God. His despair is matched only by
Mephistophiles who "saw the face of God" and is living
in everlasting torment because he will never see it again.

An occasional glimpse at the underworld in the miracle
plays becomes a sustained view in *A Knack To Know a
Knave*. The writers of miracle plays, when they reached outside their Biblical sources, sometimes reached for the under-

world. On the other hand, the writers of morality plays were able, by the very nature of their dramatized allegories, to make important use of the underworld. Contact with the underworld became an indispensable aspect of Man's temporary descent to hell; it was the moral testing ground in which he always failed. The underworld also became a vehicle' by which the dramatist could indicate the quality of his personifications. Evil characters, especially the Vice and Man in his sinful stage, invariably alluded to their association with the underworld, if they were not members of the underworld themselves. In this way the writers were able to indicate character without searching souls, the latter being impossible in true moralities. This very underworld, the symbol of evil, was able to serve also as a source of comic diversion—diversion which at times (*Wit and Wisdom, Cambises, Common Conditions*) indicates the potentialities of underworld episodes as sub-plots of serious plays. The underworld was in many respects a merry world, as a sinful world often must be. It gave the dramatists a chance to rub the audience's collective funny-bone, while the proper lessons were being taught. The underworld was, therefore, tragic and comic at the same time: tragic, because it led to Man's fall; comic, because of its essential nature and its particular treatment. The very ambiguity in the climate of opinion surrounding the Elizabethan underworld clings to the treatment of the underworld in the dramatic tradition. It is a rich ambiguity which leads to a Bellafront, a Falstaff, an Autolycus, and to all of Bartholomew Fair.

3

Thomas Dekker

Thomas Dekker is the most traditional of Elizabethan dramatists in thought and technique. Because he observed and mirrored faithfully the preoccupations of his age, and because he was essentially a hack writer who, like most hacks, unconsciously and spontaneously reflected the surface of life by conventional methods, Dekker is a revealing representative of the Elizabethan norm.[1] His treatment of the underworld clearly reveals not only the conventional climate of opinion surrounding the underworld, but the quality of Dekker's artistic achievement.

I

The most useful approach to Dekker's dramatic treatment of the underworld is by way of his prose pamphlets, because they present his views simply and clearly. A brief look at his three cony-catching pamphlets—*The Bel-Man of London, Lanthorne and Candle-Light,* and *O per se O*—is enough to discern his basic attitudes toward the underworld. Some of his other pamphlets deal with tavern life, sin, and various aspects of London low life, but in these three he is concerned directly with the underworld as a world in itself. Although much of the information he presents in these pamphlets is plagiarized, his attitudes and treatment are not.

Dekker begins the *Belman* with a eulogy of country life describing in detail a lovely grove. He enters an inn, and is allowed to watch a feast of vagabonds, who thrive on noise and drunkenness. He sees a beggar installed into the Order of the Rogue, and records the beggars' speeches and small talk. When the meal and ceremonies are over, the hostess of the inn tells Dekker what he wants to know about the rogues and lists their orders. This description and listing is taken from Thomas Harman's *A Caveat for Common Curse-tors.* Dekker leaves the inn, disgusted with country life. He returns to London, meets the Belman, whose experiences enable Dekker to tell about the cozeners and cheats of London. Most of the London material is taken from Robert Greene.

This is a bare outline of the *Belman,* which contains material plagiarized from Harman and Greene. But within this pamphlet Dekker presents his fundamental opinions about the underworld. Whenever he can, he vehemently denounces its members, whether they be wandering rogues or city sharpers. He emphasizes that they are "professed foes to the Republic, to honesty, to civility, and to all humanity." The underworld, for Dekker, is a serious danger to England and to humanity, as it is for the other dispensers of popular beliefs. Dekker's concern for England and humanity is evident in all of his work. The rogues and cozeners are "savages," whose only cure is the gallows. Dekker presents the initial pastoral scene in the *Belman* in order to contrast strikingly the peace and beauty of nature with the confusion and ugliness of the thieving beggars. A romantic strain is mingling with a realistic strain even in this hack piece of prose. The only warmth in the entire pamphlet is found in the Speaker's praise of beggary at the feast of the vagabonds.

The life of a *Begger* is the life of a souldier: he suffers hunger, & cold in winter, and heate and thirst in Sommer: he goes lowsie, hee goes lame, hees not regarded, hees not rewarded: here onely shines his glorie; The whole *Kingdome* is but his *Walke,* a whole Cittie is but his parish, in every mans kitchin is his meate drest, in every mans seller lyes his beare, and the best mens pursses keepe a penny for him to spend.[2]

The warmth, however, comes not from Dekker's sympathy for the beggar, but from his love for the soldier, a sentiment found in many of Dekker's plays. Because a substantial number of beggars were once soldiers, Dekker is careful to praise the true soldier turned beggar and to chastise, as he does in *The Roaring Girl,* the beggars who pretend participation in the wars.

In *Lanthorne and Candle-Light,* sequel to the *Belman,* Dekker continues his invective. In a prefatory letter to his patron Dekker writes:

Give mee leave to lead you by the hand into a *Wildenesse* (where are none but Monsters, whose crueltie you need not feare, because i teach the way to tame them: ugly they are in shape and divelish in conditions: yet to behold them a far off, may delight you, and to know their qualities (if ever you should come neere them) may save you from much danger.[3]

In his preface to "my owne Nation"—Dekker is always patri-
otic—he again talks about "Wilde and Barbarous Rebels . . .
in open armes against the Tranquility of the Weale publique."
He begins this pamphlet with direct plagiarism from Harman's
canting dictionary. He then presents a scene in Hell, where a
council meets to plan action against the Belman of London
who has caused trouble to a "number of the Devil's owne
kindred," for he "lookt into the secrets of the best trades that
are taught in hell." In this scene the intimate relationship
between the two *under*worlds is strikingly evident: it is a
relationship always present in Dekker's mind and in the mind
of the average Elizabethan. In this pamphlet Dekker describes what he knows much about—the cozening tricks practiced by needy poets, hack writers, brokers. He is much
closer to these goings-on than to the thieveries of rogues
and vagabonds.

O per se O is a continuation of *Lanthorne*. Here the
writer takes into his service a rogue called O per se O. He
then reveals what the rogue tells him about vagabond life.
Here again he presents bitter invective against the underworld. Here too is found a description of the fictitious Durrest
Fair, where "you shall see more rogues than ever were
whipped at a cart's arse through London, and more beggars
than ever came dropping out of Ireland. If you look upon
them, you would think you lived in Henry the Sixth's time,
and that Jack Cade and his rebellious ragmuffins were there
mustering." [4] The Jack Cade reference is in tune with Dekker's other associations of the underworld with rebellion and
disorder.

The three pamphlets, very briefly sketched, reveal that
Dekker's attitude toward the underworld conforms to the
conventional climate of opinion. To him this world was a
hell on earth, a source of disorder and confusion in the com-

monwealth. He is vehement in his denunciation of the underworld, strong in his hatred of it—and always moral. No rogue
in a Dekker pamphlet is allowed to repent, although conversion was a common practice in rogue literature. Dekker's
anger and hatred stem from the important fact that the citizens of London and England were the victims of the city and
country thieves. Indeed, it is his love for the citizens that
puts him closer to the official enemies of the underworld than
to the rogue pamphleteers. Whereas Greene, a Bohemian,
can see the charm as well as the harm of the underworld,
Dekker, a member of the bourgeoisie and a lover of the
citizen class, can see only the harm. This joint sympathy for
the citizen world and antipathy toward the underworld is
evident whenever Dekker sounds the base string.

II

Dekker's most significant dramatic treatment of the underworld begins in the year 1604 with *The Honest Whore*. Before this Dekker wrote a number of plays which are distin-
guished, in the first place, by a romantic tendency—treatment
of folklore, allegory, pseudo-history—and, in the second place,
by an emphasis on the healthy emotions of honest laborers.
In these plays he shows little dramatic interest in low life,
an interest which is often considered an intrinsic part of
his particular genius. In these early plays there are no underworld characters. However, they do contain scattered allusions to the underworld which indicate Dekker's attitude
before his treatment of the underworld in play or pamphlet.

Old Fortunatus, based on a German folk tale and related
to the morality play, contains several references to the underworld. Shadow, the servant of the sons of Fortunatus, states:
"Theres no man but loves one of these three beastes, a Horse,

a Hound, or a Whore; the Horse by his goodwill, has his head ever in the maunger; the Whore with your ill will has her hand ever in your purse; and a hungry Dogge eates durtie puddings." [5] In this one sentence Dekker associates the most important member of the underworld in all his works, the whore, with a beast, and he alludes to her thieving habits. Shadow, in the same scene, comparing the rest of the world to his home Cyprus asserts, after a series of comparisons: "I confesse you shall meete more fooles, and asses, and knaves abroad then at home (yet God be thanked we have pretty store of all) but for Punckes, we put them downe" (II,2,408-410). Dekker, like the London officials, is ever conscious of the number of whores in London. The other underworld references come from the mouth of Andelocia, the younger son of Fortunatus, the son who is in the moral world of the play the "brother Vice." When he brings Agripyne to the desert to seduce her, she calls him a devil, to which he answers, since she stole his magic purse: "Indeed the divel and the pick-purse should alwaies flie together, (for they are sworne brothers)" (IV,1,4-5). The Devil-underworld association is ever present in Dekker's plays. Andelocia shows his familiarity with thieves when he asks Agripyne for the purse—"You know the thiefes salutation, Stand and deliver. So, this is mine, and these yours: Ile teach you to live by the sweate of other mens browes" (V,2,5-7). That thieves live by the sweat of other men's brows is one of the reasons for Dekker's antipathy toward them. In earlier scenes Andelocia talks of cozening and of "a Conie taken napping in a Pursenet." His speech indicates his familiarity with the activities of the underworld, throwing a dark light on his already dark character. This is a typical practice in the morality tradition, as Chapter 2 has demonstrated. Andelocia's brother Ampedo, "my brother Virtue," stands in direct contrast to Andelocia and utters this statement early in the play: "I am not enamoured of this painted Idoll,/ This strumpet world." Andelocia is very much in love with the strumpet world, as his actions in the play and his underworld-associative language indicate. Virtue and Vice are clearly marked in this romantic morality tale. The *idea* of the underworld helps to produce this clarity, as it did in the earlier moralities.

The Whore of Babylon[6] also enables Dekker to moralize, and once again the characters clearly represent vice and virtue, falsehood and truth. Allusions to the underworld significantly contribute to the moral contrasts in the play. Dekker is ostensibly attacking Roman Catholicism, which he represents as the Empress of Babylon, the titular Whore of Babylon. Throughout this allegorical drama he plays upon the idea of whore. The disgust with the whores of the underworld that is found in his pamphlets and later plays in this play has as its object the sluttish personification of Rome. She is called a harlot, a strumpet, a purple whore. Her skin is "spotted with foule disease"; her Babylonian synagogues are called stews. She even has a bawd, Falsehood, about whom Plain-dealing says this: "This villanous drab is bawd, now I remember, to the Whore of *Babylon;* and weele never leave her, till shee be carted: her face is full of those red pimples with drinking Aquavite, the common drinke of all bawdes" (IV,1,70-73). These are the characteristics of most of Dekker's bawds.

The Whore of Babylon rants against Titania, the Fairie Queen (Elizabeth), and commands her kings to go to the Fairie Land and woo the Queen "so she will kneele and doe us reverence." The Satan image is suggested when she tells the kings to flatter Titania "like to serpents." The association of whore with Devil seems inevitable. The whore is also related to disorder and chaos—*Confusion* is written on the brow of the Whore of Babylon. Although she is essentially a religious foe of England, she stands also as an enemy to England's national prosperity. Her ministers attempt to cause civil discontent. The Whore of Babylon takes her place in the underworld of Dekker's plays and pamphlets as a source of chaos in the commonwealth. She is the symbol of the hellish confusion which England must combat.

Whereas *Old Fortunatus* and *The Whore of Babylon,* both strongly affected by the morality tradition, are examples of Dekker's treatment of folklore and allegory, *Patient Grissil* and *The Shoemakers' Holiday* present the healthy emotions of working people. *The Shoemakers' Holiday,* the liveliest and healthiest of Dekker's plays, is especially important to this study because in it one gets the best sense of Dekker's great love of the burgeoisie. Forgiveness and love and patriotism and pride in work are part of the play's atmosphere. The play has no underworld character and no important reference to the underworld. "Nothing is purposed but mirth," says Dekker, and mirth is what he gives his audience. The joy in life is the keynote of the play, a joy only hinted at in Dekker's other plays. Dekker presents no elements to destroy this joy. The Ralph-Jane story is presented with a sweet kind of sadness, the audience knowing that Jane will always be true to her husband. Jane's display of loyalty for Ralph is unquestionably a Dekkerian ideal for citizen conduct, against which the behavior of citizens' wives in other plays must be measured. Once Lacy becomes an apprentice of Simon Eyre, the audience has no fear that Lacy will not get his Rose. An apprentice of Simon Eyre must be happy! A reader of all Dekker's plays, in and out of collaboration, can discern why this play is the healthiest and liveliest—Dekker is portraying the people, the world, he loves most, and he is dealing with them exclusively. (The King is absorbed in the Eyre atmos-

phere and Lacy becomes a shoemaker's apprentice.) The play
contains no underworld character and only four unimportant
references to the underworld. This absence is significant.
No underworld taint affects the play's atmosphere. The air
is clean; the characters are clean; the craftsman-citizen world
is clean. An appreciation of Dekker's love of the bourgeoisie
is the very basis for understanding his mind and art.

The loyalty of a woman to a man is the main theme of
Patient Grissil, which Dekker wrote in collaboration with
Henry Chettle and William Haughton. The Grissil story, in
which the patience of Grissil is tried by her husband, is probably Dekker's, as is the sub-plot—the strife between a Welsh
knight, Sir Owen ap Meredith, and his Welsh bride, Gwenthyan, in which Gwenthyan tries the patience of Sir Owen
by acting the shrew. Only in the scenes relating to the
Welsh knight do references to the underworld appear, but
these are fleeting and unimportant. In Act IV, scene 3,
however, a company of beggars occupies the stage. Gwenthyan, to annoy Sir Owen, invites beggars into the house to
eat all the food so that Sir Owen's guests will have nothing
to eat when they arrive. The stage-direction reads: "A
drunken feast, they quarrel and grow drunke, and pocket
up the meate, the dealing of Cannes like a set at Mawe." One
is reminded of the beggar banquet in the *Belman,* where
drunkenness and quarreling is also associated with beggars.
When leaving the feast, a beggar says: "Come you roagues,
lets goe tag and rag, cut and long taile, I am victualed for a
month, God bo'y Madame, pray God Sir Owen and you may
fall out every day: Is there any harme in this nowe? hey
tri-lill, give the dog a loafe, fill tother pot you whoore and
God save the Duke" (IV,3,41-45). This is playful, to be
sure, but it is noteworthy that these parasites are benefiting
from a domestic quarrel—the underworld's relationship to

disorder is evident even in a domestic situation. In this scene
Dekker also uses the underworld to try the patience of a
sympathetic character. This will be one of the functions of
Dekker's dramatic underworld in later plays.

Satiromastix, Dekker's answer to Jonson's *Poetaster*, contains only a few allusions to the underworld, all by Captain
Tucca. In Act I he refers to the poets as "bastards of nine
whoores, the Muses," and in Act IV calls the Muses "nine
common wenches." He ridicules Horace's (Jonson's) struggle
to finish an ode: "His wittes are somewhat hard bound: the
Puncke his Muse has sore labour ere the whore be delivered:
the poore saffron-cheeke Sun-burnt Gipsie wants Phisicke"
(I,2,366-68). Tucca tells Horace why he chastises him:
"Because thou cryest ptrooh at worshipfull Cittizens, and
cal'st them Flat-caps, Cuckolds, and banckrupts, and modest
and vertuous wives punckes and cockatrices" (IV,3,194-96).
Dekker clearly allies himself with the citizens and citizens'
wives, and calls upon the underworld merely to help him
poke fun at Jonson.

The history play, *Sir Thomas Wyatt*, need only be mentioned. This collaboration between Dekker and Webster—
Stoll attributes almost everything to Dekker[7]—contains only
one underworld allusion. Pembroke asserts that he "was
talking with a crue of vagabonds that lagd at Wiats taile."
Vagabonds were potential mobs with grievances against the
state and could easily be aroused to rebel behind some leader.
In this play the leader is Sir Thomas Wyatt.

The underworld in Dekker's early plays is not a specific
dramatic world. It is neither a structural entity nor a source
of character. It is, however, an image, especially in *Old
Fortunatus* and *The Whore of Babylon*, associated with vice,
disorder, and hell. Thus, up to 1604 Dekker has no *dramatic*
interest in the underworld, but with *The Honest Whore,*

Westward Ho, Northward Ho and *The Roaring Girl* he
plunges into the muck of London life. He represents on the
boards immoral men and women, brothels, taverns, Bridewell,
Bedlam.[8] He clearly translates his attitude toward the underworld into dramatic action.

III

The Honest Whore (1604)[9] is the first and best of Dekker's plays directly dealing with the underworld. In it he
presents underworld characters, significant comments on the
underworld, and his first use of the underworld as a world
in direct contrast to the citizen world. There is no known
source for the play. The conversion of a whore is an Elizabethan commonplace in drama and prose pamphlet. Dekker
need only have looked at one of Greene's conycatching
pamphlets, *A Disputation between a Hee Connycatcher and a
Shee Conny-catcher,* to find "The Conversion of an English
Courtezan," a first-person narrative about a girl turned
wanton (because, as in the moralities, her parents spared the
rod), her whorish affairs, and her final conversion. The
conversion of this whore is caused by an honest clothier who
reminds her that God is forever watching this world and that
whores are eternally damned. She is affected by his talk,
gives up whoredom, marries the clothier, and lives happily
ever after. The conversion of Dekker's whore, Bellafront, is
also caused by the speech of a man she loves, but the re-
semblance ends there, for Bellafront does not marry the man
she loves and lives happily never after. Dekker's idea of conversion, based on a strong moral bias, is far different from
Greene's. It is the focal point for any discussion of Dekker's
attitude toward the underworld.

In the play's first scene, Hippolito, lamenting the death of his beloved Infelice, chastises "this adulterous bawdy world." Although for him, in this moment of grief, the entire world is adulterous and bawdy, for Dekker only the court world and the underworld are such—the citizen world, represented by Candido and his circle, is clean and healthy. Hippolito's statement and the entire first act, with its comments by various characters about whores and the state of morality in Milan, set the tone for most of the play's machinations and prepare for the introduction of the main character, Bellafront, in Act II, scene 1. In the beginning of this scene Bellafront is a popular courtesan. At the end of the scene she has become the Honest Whore. That such a sudden conversion is believable is a credit to Dekker's ability to characterize. That the conversion occurs in the second act of a play that will discuss this conversion for eight more acts is an indication of Dekker's purpose. The converted harlots in other plays of the Elizabethan period and in Dekker's later plays announce their conversion in Act V; the play then ends and all's well. The conversion of Bellafront is the *beginning*—it sets off a chain of miseries which Bellafront must suffer. She must pay for the sins she committed in the underworld she rejects. Dekker's antipathy to the underworld is too strong, at least at the writing of this play, to allow for an easy conversion. Dekker, unlike the other rogue pamphleteers, never mentions conversion in his angry exposés of the underworld. This play, coming before the pamphlets, suggests why—the road to cleanliness and moral health is a treacherous one; only the most enduring can traverse it. In this important respect Dekker is a link between the morality tradition and the Elizabethan tradition, for the moralities had already dramatized the difficult path to virtue.

Bellafront is an experienced witty prostitute, who is able to handle men with the assurance of a Meretrix. Her word-play with her servant Roger, "a panderly Sixpenny Rascall," her talk with the gallants who visit her, and her anger toward Matheo all display a woman set in the ways of harlotry. When she speaks with Hippolito, however, the soft side of her nature becomes evident. She sincerely desires to be loved by one man.

> O my Stars!
> Had I but met with one kind gentleman,
> That would have purchacde sin alone, to himselfe,
> For his owne private use, although scarce proper:
> Indifferent hansome: meetly legd and thyed:
> And my allowance reasonable—yfaith,
> According to my body—by my troth,
> I would have bin as true unto his pleasures,
> Yea, and as loyall to his afternoones,
> As ever a poore gentlewoman could be.
>
>   (II,1,267-276)

She sees Hippolito as that potential lover. He, aided by his speech against harlotry, causes her to resolve to turn "pure honest." In Hippolito's tirade Dekker is able to present his own hatred for the whore. The speech is too long to quote in full; these excerpts will indicate Dekker's venom:

> You have no soule,
> That makes you wey so light: heavens treasure bought it,
> And halfe a crowne hath sold it; for your body,
> Its like the common shoare, that still receives
> All the townes filth. The sin of many men
> Is within you, and thus much I suppose,
> That if all your committers stood in ranke,
> Theide make a lane, (in which your shame might dwell)
> And with their spaces reach from hence to hell.
> Nay, shall I urge it more, there has bene knowne,

> As many by one harlot, maym'd and dismembered,
> As would ha stuft an Hospitall: this I might
> Apply to you, and perhaps do you right:
> O y'are as base as any beast that beares,
> Your body is ee'ne hirde, and so are theirs.
>
> Me thinks a toad is happier than a whore,
> That with one poison swells, with thousands more,
> The other stocks her veines: harlot? fie! fie,
> You are the miserablest Creatures breathing,
> The very slaves of nature.
>
> Oh you have damnation without pleasure for it!
> Such is the state of Harlots. To conclude,
> When you are old, and can well paynt no more,
> You turne Bawd, and are then worse then before:
> Make use of this: farewell.
>
> (II,1,322-336;360-64;419-423)

The whore, for Dekker, is a damned filthy diseased beast, and a menace to all who have contact with her. Despite the vehemence of this speech, Bellafront's first attempt at self-examination, when Hippolito leaves, brings forth this question:

> Yet why should sweet *Hipolito* shun mine eyes;
> For whose true love I would become pure-honest,
> Hate the worlds mixtures, and the smiles of gold:
> Am I not fayre? Why should he flye me then?
>
> (II,1,430-33)

The harlot is not so affected by the subject matter and tone of the tirade as by Hippolito's reaction to her, personally. Bellafront, reviewing the words of Hippolito in her mind, seems to *discover* that her harlotry is the cause for Hippolito's disgust.

Hipolito hath spyed some ugly blemish,
Eclipsing all my beauties: I am foule:
Harlot! I, that' the spot that taynts my soule.
(II,1,441-443)

Her vanity is a strong part of her nature and love is the impulse for her conversion. With this slight touch Dekker demonstrates his ability to present an essentially truthful depiction of character. Bellafront, now aware of her tainted soul, attempts to stab herself, but is stopped by Hippolito. She resolves to win his love in some way, and ends the scene with these words: "Would all the Whores were as honest now, as I." The rest of Part I and all of Part II demonstrate the truth of this assertion.

From this point on Dekker is able to use Bellafront as his mouthpiece of morality. From her lips comes his invective against sin, whores, bawds, panders, and whoremongering gallants. This is as it should be. Charles Lamb, in a note concerning a passage in the second part of this play, states "that a worn-out Sinner is sometimes found to make the best Declaimer against Sin. The same high-seasoned descriptions which in his unregenerate state served to inflame his appetites, in his new province of a Moralist will serve him (a little turned) to expose the enormity of those appetites in other men." [10] This speech, chastising her bawd, Mistress Fingerlock, is typical of her new morality and emphasizes that she is an excellent "Declaimer against Sin":

Hence, thou our sexes monster, poysonous Bawd,
Lusts Factor, and damnations Orator,
Gossip of hell, were all the Harlots sinnes
Which the whole world conteynes, numbred together,
Thine far exceeds them all; of all the creatures
That ever were created, thou art basest:

What serpent would beguile thee of thy Office?
It is detestable: for thou liv'st
Upon the dregs of Harlots, guard'st the dore,
Whilst couples goe to dauncing: O course devill!
Thou art the bastards curse, thou brandst his birth,
The lechers French disease; for thou dry-suckst him:
The Harlots poyson, and thine owne confusion.
                                        (III,2,30-42)

Indeed, Bellafront has performed, as Matheo states, "one of *Hercules* labours"—a whore has turned honest.

Bellafront attempts by strategems to win Hippolito, and when the play ends in Bethlem Monasterie, she even feigns madness (an underworld trick of the Abram man), but to no avail. Hippolito has his Infelice; Bellafront accepts Matheo, the man who turned her whore, who claims that he has been "Cony-catcht, guld." Part I ends. Bellafront's conversion has not been too difficult—she is abused by the bawd, pander, gallants, and her future husband; she loses the one man she loves; she accepts the unscrupulous Matheo for her husband. Dekker must write another play to test the sincerity of her conversion.

In Part II Bellafront suffers with a worthless husband who himself hovers on the brink of the underworld—he dices, whores, and cheats; he forces Bellafront to beg for him; her gown is taken from her back to be pawned; she is threatened with physical violence. Matheo even asks her to turn whore again because he needs the money. Bellafront, in misery, exclaims: "A thousand sorrowes strike/ At one poore heart." Her situation is wretched. Orlando Friscobaldo's appearance causes her additional anguish, for she must keep her husband and father at peace with one another. Then a new temptation, the greatest of all, arises to test her honesty. Hippolito has become a "muttonmonger" and wishes to seduce Bellafront. He argues for harlotry, just as he argued against it in Part I. The man who caused her to convert, her saviour, is now her tempter. But she resists and presents a speech against harlotry equal in moral fervor to his former speech. In short, Dekker makes her new way of life a continuous trial—a trial which ennobles her nature, a trial in many ways similar to the trial of the legendary whore, Thais, who also turned honest and had to suffer greatly before she gained Paradise. However, Dekker's whore remains, at the end of the play, with her worthless husband; and Dekker gives no indication that Matheo will ever change. No relief of her misery is in sight.

The conversion of Bellafront is central to the play and to Dekker's attitude toward the underworld. Dekker puts his main character through the miseries of a hell on earth. His treatment of Bellafront is influenced by his strict and severe morality. He causes the audience to feel genuine sympathy for Bellafront's suffering, but the audience at the same time realizes that her being sinned against has been caused by her sinning. In the course of the two parts of *The Honest Whore* Bellafront takes on the characteristics of a Jane. Her citizen virtues, especially her conjugal loyalty, makes her a heroine; but her trials are not part of a holiday atmosphere. The misery of Bellafront seems everlasting.

Bellafront is, of course, not the only underworld character in the two parts of *The Honest Whore*. Roger, the pander, and Mistress Fingerlock, the bawd, are found in Part I. Lieutenant Bots, a pander, Madam Horseleech, a bawd— "burnt at fourteene, seven times whipt, sixe times carted, nine times duck'd search'd by some hundred and fifty Constables" —and the three harlots in Bridewell are found in Part II. All of these are the objects of Dekker's abuse, and all are

presented with striking realism. Bots will be whipped and
punished, for as the First Master of Bridewell says:

> The pander is more dangerous to a State,
> Then is the common Thiefe, and tho our lawes
> Lie heavier on the Thief, yet that the Pander
> May know the Hangmans ruffe should fit him too,
> Therefore he's set to beat Hempe.
>
> (V,2,246-250)

The typical rogue-pamphlet sentiment that the underworld
is a danger to the commonwealth is again put forth by
Dekker. The three Bridewell whores are all vile; they represent three different kinds of whore. Doll Target is dressed
as a gentlewoman and denies that she is a whore. (Doll
Hornet in *Northward Ho* will disguise as a gentlewoman for
cony-catching purposes.) Penelope Whorehound is dressed
as a citizen's wife. When asked her name she says: "Penelope
Whorehound, I come of the *Whorehounds.*" She complains
that when she goes among the citizens' wives they jeer at
her, and when she goes among "the Loose-bodied Gownes"
they "cry a pox" on her. The third harlot, Catyryna Bounti-
nall, is a swaggering whore, proud of her profession—"you'll
creepe up to my placket, and yee cood but attaine the
honour." Each will be punished. Roger and Mistress Fingerlock will, however, thrive "so long as there be any Tavernes
and bawdy houses in Millain."

In addition, throughout both parts, Dekker refers to the
practices and antics of the members of the underworld, practices which he directly discusses in the pamphlets.

The underworld in *The Honest Whore* is dramatically important. Its members are realistically represented on the
boards; its vices are exposed; its essential filth and disorder

are emphasized. Dekker surrounds the underworld with a whole complex of attitudes which were already observed in his earlier plays and in his pamphlets, but which are dramatized in both parts of this play. The underworld, however, does not exist alone. It serves as a moral reflector of and interacts with the other two worlds of the play, the court world and the citizen world. This interaction significantly influences the structure of the play.

Most critics of Dekker's dramaturgy agree that his work is faulty. A. H. Bullen asserts that Dekker "usually showed a reckless indifference in the management of his plots." [11] Swinburne writes of Dekker's "besetting sin of laxity, his want of seriousness and steadiness, his idle, shambling, shifty way of writing." [12] F. E. Pierce calls Dekker "one of the most careless writers of a careless age." [13] Ellis-Fermor says that he is "unconscious of art." [14] Dekker probably would have admitted all of these shortcomings. The Preface to *If This Be Not a Good Play, The Devil Is In It* directly expresses some of his aims as a playwright. He emphasizes the importance of language and the stirring of emotions, specifically stating that emotions must be so arranged as to present striking contrasts. This kind of emphasis may not produce careful and truthful depiction of character, but it can produce good theater. In *The Honest Whore* it produced both, for Dekker was able to contrast strikingly the two aspects of Bellafront's character in one scene and to make this contrast both truthful to her character and theatrically effective. In fact, *The Honest Whore* is an exception to all of the generalizations about Dekker's faulty craftsmanship. Swinburne himself states that

of all Dekker's works, "The Honest Whore" comes nearest to some reasonable degree of unity and harmony in conception and construction; his besetting vice of reckless and sluttish incoherence has here done less than usual to deform the proportions and deface the impression of his design. Indeed, the connection of the two serious plots in the first part is a rare example of dexterous and happy simplicity in composition: the comic underplot of the patient man and shrewish wife is more loosely attached by a slighter thread of relation to these two main stories, but is so amusing in its light and facile play of inventive merriment and harmless mischief as to need no further excuse.[15]

The connection between the two serious plots is, indeed, dexterously handled. In fact, they mesh so smoothly that a strong case can be made that they are *one* serious plot. Bellafront's story is directly involved with the Hippolito-Infelice story. The events of one directly influence the events of the other. One need only mention that the courtier Matheo is married to a converted whore, that the gallants were the customers of Bellafront, that Carolo and Lodovico are associated with Bots and Madam Horseleech, that Bellafront helps to resolve the Hippolito-Infelice plot. The underplot, concerning the trials of the patient Candido of the citizen world, is more loosely connected to the main plot, *but* the "thread of relation" is not slight—that is, the two plots rarely touch, but the light thrown on the main plot by the sub-plot is a very revealing one. And when the plots do touch, they *clash*—an effect which Dekker works for and which in itself is a comment on Dekker's attitude toward the underworld and his attitude toward the citizen world.

Candido is "a grave citizen" and the "mirror of patience." He is "so milde, so affable, so suffering, that nothing indeede can moove him." His wife Viola cannot endure his patience and tries in many ways to vex him—but she cannot. The gallants visit his shop, also attempting to vex him—but they cannot. Viola, as a last maneuver, calls in officers to carry Candido to the madhouse—but even in the madhouse, where the complications of Part I are resolved, Candido remains patient. It is in the madhouse that Candido presents his famous speech, in which the sentiments expressed seem very close to Dekker's heart.

> Patience my Lord; Why tis the soule of peace:
> Of all the vertues tis neerst kin to heaven.
> It makes men looke like Gods; the best of men
> That ere wore earth about him, was a sufferer,
> A soft, meeke, patient, humble, tranquill spirit,
> The first true Gentleman that ever breathd;
> The stock of *Patience* then cannot be poore,
> All it desires it has; what Monarch more?
> (V,2,489-496)

The Duke, at the end of Part I, praises Candido's patience and says that Candido "shall teach our court to shine." In Part II Candido continues to display his patience. This time he has a new wife, who at first is strong-minded but learns to submit to her husband. The gallants again try to ruffle Candido, and again they are thwarted. When he goes to Matheo's house to see some pieces of lawn he finds that he is in the company of a bawd and panderer and that the pieces of lawn are stolen goods. He is apprehended by officers and taken to Bridewell, where the plots of Part II are resolved. Candido again receives the praise of the Duke.

> Thou hast taught the Citty patience, now our Court
> Shall be thy Spheare, where from thy good report,
> Rumours this truth unto the world shall sing,
> A Patient man's a Pattern for a King.
> (V,2,494-497)

The Candido story is the source of most of the play's humor.
But it cannot be dismissed merely as a piece of merriment.
Candido is, essentially, a Dekker hero. He is the representative of the citizen world, the world to which Dekker is most
attached. He displays the qualities of industriousness, gen-
erosity, and patience. He is comically patient, to be sure, but
Dekker forgets the comedy when Candido presents his speech
on Patience and when the Duke considers him "a Patterne
for a King." It is the very quality of patience that Bellafront
displays in both parts of *The Honest Whore*. She, however,
is heroic in her patience. Candido's comment that "the best
of men . . . was a sufferer" applies to Bellafront almost as
much as it does to Jesus. Jesus suffered for the sins of the
world; Bellafront suffers for her own sins as a member of
the underworld. *The Honest Whore* is basically a dramatic
study of patience. To dismiss the Candido story with a chuckle
is to neglect a significant element in this study.[16]

The Candido story is also important in another respect.
It clearly demonstrates Dekker's interest in and attitude toward
the citizen world. That the underworld and the court world
mingle has already been observed. The citizen and court
worlds also meet, but only in business affairs and when the
gallants attempt to annoy Candido. The citizen world and
the underworld make no contact in Part I. In Part II they
meet twice, with interesting results. Carolo, a courtier, gives
the bawd and pander money to arrange a meeting between
Candido's wife and himself. When Bots presents Carolo's
proposition to the bride, she emphatically scorns him, calls him
"an arrant knave," and leaves his company. The virtuous
wife of the citizen Candido utterly rejects the underworld's
representative. Just as the play contains a parallel between
the patience of Candido and the patience of Bellafront, so
too it contains a parallel between the virtue of Candido's wife

and the virtue of Bellafront—both cannot be seduced, both
display conjugal loyalty, like Jane in *Shoemakers' Holiday*.
Candido's bride and the honest whore are one in faithfulness,
with Bellafront having the harder trial because she loved her
seducer and because her husband is worthless. Bellafront,
once a member of the underworld, in her moral recovery
gathers to herself qualities of the citizen world.

The second meeting between the two worlds occurs when
Candido goes to Matheo's house to see the pieces of lawn.
The bawd and pander are there. Candido, not knowing
Mistress Horseleech is a bawd, is introduced to her. She
politely kisses him, which causes him to mutter, "Sh'as a
breath stinkes worse then fifty Polecats. Sir, a word, is she
a Lady?" He is able to smell her bawdiness. When he is
told that she is a bawd he is ready to leave the house, but is
forced to remain and drink healths to her, which thoroughly
disgusts him. The aversion of Dekker's citizen to a representative of the underworld is strikingly evident throughout the
scene. The two worlds meet, but the citizen world is repelled.

By its lack of contact with the underworld in Part I and
by its two clashes with the underworld in Part II, the citizen
world is presented by Dekker as a clean, healthy world, in
which the daily business of living is carried on with zest and
with an absence of vice. Dekker demonstrates in this play,
as he does in his pamphlets, that he loves the citizen world
and its virtues, that he hates the underworld and its vices.
He clearly distinguishes black from white, even when Bellafront travels from black to white. In *The Honest Whore* the
strictness of Dekker's morality seems to dictate a strictness in
handling plot. This is his best constructed drama. Dekker
acquired, if only in this play, Candido's patience.

The Honest Whore is Dekker's most conscientious effort.
When he put it behind him, he left with it his strict adher-

ence to a citizen morality. *Westward Ho* and *Northward Ho,* both collaborations with Webster and both acted before a private-theater audience, present the three worlds found in *The Honest Whore.* In these plays, however, the worlds mesh; the morality is easy.

The plot of *Westward Ho,* like that of *Northward Ho,* deals with the intrigue between gallants and citizens' wives, helped along by the underworld. Dekker's traditional distaste for the underworld is essentially the same here as in *The Honest Whore,* but his use of the underworld is far different. For the underworld in *Westward Ho* provides Dekker with a norm for a satirical attack on the citizens,[17] which leads to nothing less than a changed concept of the bourgeoisie. The abuse that the jealous industrious citizens and their fun-loving wives receive is provoked by the relationship of the citizens with the underworld. The three citizens, Honeysuckle, Tenterhook, and Wafer, are customers of Luce, an experienced whore, who runs a thriving trade with the help of one of Dekker's most disgusting bawds, Birdlime. That the citizens are patrons of the underworld indicates that Dekker is tampering with the citizen virtues he holds so high. Candido was repelled by the underworld; the citizens in this play wish to embrace it. The stern morality displayed in *The Honest Whore* is slackening. In connection with the citizens' wives, the pattern of *The Honest Whore* is completely reversed. Throughout the play there are surprising parallels of attitude between the bawd, the whore, and the citizens' wives. They all are coarse, but they will not endure coarseness in others. They all affect virtue. They all chastise tobacco-smoking and drunkenness. They all are basically not moral—the whore and bawd play with men for pay, the wives play with gallants for merriment. Whereas in *The Honest Whore* Bellafront took on the qualities of that play's citizen world, thereby demonstrating a true conversion, in this play the citizen world acquires the qualities of the underworld. This is seen even in the most fleeting lines. Mistress Wafer tells Mistress Tenterhook that she wishes her "the fortune to change thy name often." Her reason: "For theeves and widdowes love to shift names, and make sweet use of it so." When Justiano tells his wife that she was lucky to have received the jewels of the lecherous Earl, he exclaims: "Was it ever heard that such tyrings, were brought away from a Lord by any wench but thee *Moll,* without paying, unlesse the wench connycatcht him?" (IV,2,190-92). The methods of the underworld are not unknown or repugnant to these citizens.

That citizens visit the house of a whore and that citizens' wives imitate whores and bawds presents a reversal of the strict moral pattern found in *The Honest Whore.* It is true that at the play's end the wives display a change of attitude. They cheat the gallants—"They shall know that Cittizens wives have wit enough to out strip twenty such gulls." The wives are merry and wanton, but "pure about the heart." Dekker's love of the bourgeoisie still seems to emerge, but the stern moralist has been corrupted. However, his *basic* pamphlet morality did not change, as some of his later plays indicate. Therefore, one must look for other causes for his reversal, in *Westward Ho,* of the traditional morality. Any or all of three causes are probable—the nature of the audience, Dekker's hack tendencies, his collaboration with Webster.

Alfred Harbage has *The Honest Whore* and the *Ho* plays specifically in mind when he states that "the same authors who wrote amiably of commercialized vice for Paul's provide exposés and denunciations for the Fortune." [18] To please was Dekker's constant aim. His desire to entertain the audience at Paul's, who would enjoy a satirical attack on the bourgeoisie and whose own moral standards were less exacting than those of the middle-class, perhaps caused him to compromise his moral position.

In addition, his collaboration with Webster may have affected his outlook in the *Ho* plays. Scholars dealing with this collaboration agree that Dekker was the "guiding spirit" in both *Westward Ho* and *Northward Ho*.[19] There is little doubt that Dekker wrote most of each play. But the exact nature of any collaboration cannot be demonstrated, even though a battery of valid tests can assign particular scenes and speeches to one dramatist or the other. It seems logical to assume that Dekker, the older, more experienced dramatist influenced Webster the apprentice. Yet, in the light of Dekker's hack tendencies and what seems to be a nature willing to compromise in matters of theater, this assumption could be qualified. Can one be sure that Webster gave Dekker no satiric impulse, an impulse worked upon by Dekker's own mind and art? Stoll applauds "the originality, the strong innate bent, of a mind" like Webster's "that could develop . . . in so different a direction from its master's." [20] He suggests, however, that perhaps some scenes assigned to Dekker "may have sprung from the youthful imitation and self-effacement of Webster." But is it not possible that in connection with the satire of the citizens the "strong innate bent" of Webster, although youthful, influenced an older dramatist who often effaced himself? This is in the realm of conjecture, but it is a useful speculation because it conforms to the impression one gets of the theatrically compromising Dekker and helps in part to explain Dekker's new concept of the bourgeoisie. Dekker's attitude seems to depend much upon his collaborator's attitude, as his later collaborations clearly indicate.

Northward Ho conforms to the new moral pattern set up by *Westward Ho,* and once again the underworld is a revealing focus for demonstrating this pattern. Doll Hornet is the underworld character who receives most of Dekker's attention in *Northward Ho*. She is a vociferous whore, often reminding one of Doll Tearsheet. Through her words and action Dekker presents many tricks of the trade. She is an experienced cony-catcher, and she has accomplices in her profession. Act II, scene 1, presents her entire crew in action; the scene is a dramatic representation of some of the subject matter in Dekker's pamphlets. Doll, by disguising as a gentlewoman, is able to cony-catch Hans Van Belch, Allum, Captain Jenkins, and Philip Bellamont. She, like Bellafront, falls in love—with, of all people, Dekker's representation of Chapman: Bellamont, the hoary poet. Perhaps Dekker is here poking gentle fun at Chapman whose appearance alone can convert whores. But Bellamont emerges as Dekker's spokesman against the underworld, and expresses Dekker's traditional distaste for whores. He calls Doll "a common undertaker," for she promises "nothing but watchet eyes, bombast calves, and false perywigs." He suggests this as a panacea for the city:

I wud some honest Butcher would begge all the queanes and knaves ith citty and carry them into some other Country, they'd sell better than Beefes and Calves: what a vertuous Citty would this bee then!

(III,1,110-113)

He associates the whore with the devil, as Dekker often does, when he asks Doll—"what saies the divell to al the world, for Ime sure thou art carnally possest with him." He chastises his son for being one of Doll's many customers: "If nothing but raw mutton can diet thee, looke to live like a foole and a slave, and to die like a begger and a knave" (I,3, 183-185). This is the fate of most men who deal with whores.

In short, Bellamont's complete aversion to the underworld is
Dekker's aversion.[21] Yet, despite the abuse that Doll Hornet
receives, she is placed on the road to respectability. Dekker
uses a typical Middleton trick of marrying his whore off to
an unsympathetic character. He did this in *The Honest
Whore* but the difference here indicates a shifting morality.
Bellafront's marriage to Matheo was presented as punishment
for the whore, whereas Doll's marriage to Fetherstone is punishment for Fetherstone, who thinks Doll is a rich ward.
Instead of being punished, the underworld is used as an
instrument for punishment. Captain Jenkins, one of the victims of Doll's cony-catching days, tells Fetherstone: "Your
wife is a Tilt-boate, any man or oman may goe in her for
money; shee's a Cunny-catcher." Her other victims ask for the
money she stole from them. Doll is still vociferous: "Out you
base scums, come you to disgrace mee in my wedding shoes?"
However, she does vow faithfulness to Fetherstone, who re-
conciles himself to his fate. Doll's conversion is easy. When
one considers that the same dramatist who presented Bellafront presented Doll Hornet, only one conclusion can be
drawn—Dekker's stern morality could be compromised under
specific theatrical conditions.

Northward Ho, like *The Honest Whore,* has a scene in
Bedlam, where a mad bawd is one of the inmates. She loves
aquavite, swears by her virginity, and denies ever being in
Bridewell. She is, in short, one of Dekker's traditional bawds.
Her appearance is very brief, but it serves as a distinct focus
for summing up Dekker's use of the underworld in the play.
She states her preference for "your *London* Prentice" and
"taylors" as customers. The citizen-underworld relationship
sheds a disparaging light on the citizens, with the underworld
again providing the moral norm for a satiric thrust. The
citizen world in *Northward Ho* has no "hero" like Candido

and no outstanding virtues. The citizens still remain Dekker's favorites ("Sfoote ther's neare a Gentleman of them
all shall gull a Citizen, and think to go scot-free.") but his
treatment of them has significantly changed. In the *Ho*
plays, because of Dekker's hack tendencies and perhaps because of his collaboration with Webster, one witnesses a
clear breakdown of a traditional stern morality—a striking
example of expediency undermining genuine belief.

This breakdown becomes more complete in Dekker's next
play, *The Roaring Girl,* a collaboration with Middleton.
Whereas in the *Ho* plays the underworld was a hateful and
sinful world, and therefore a norm for satire against the
citizens, in *The Roaring Girl* the underworld is romanticized.
Mary Frith, alias Moll Cutpurse, is a true Elizabethan underworld character, a notorious thief who even had to do penance
at St. Paul's Cross in 1612. Here, one would think, is the
proper object of Dekkerian abuse. In this play, however,
Moll is completely whitewashed. Which of the collaborators
initially conceived the idea of making a heroine out of a
famous cutpurse is, of course, difficult to ascertain, and has
produced differing scholarly opinions. To George R. Price,
"Dekker has almost nothing to do with the depiction of
Moll." [22] On the other hand, Richard H. Barker believes
Middleton contributed to the portrayal of Moll, "but the
point of view is always Dekker's." [23] Middleton's words in the
Epistle to the Reader—" 'Tis the excellency of a Writer, to
leave things better than he finds 'em."—seem to indicate that
the charitable view of Moll originated with him, but both
dramatists obviously accept the new Moll and defend her
throughout the play. The defense and romanticization of a
thief runs counter to Dekker's traditional attitude toward the
underworld, but once again the pressure of compromise has
caused him to deviate from the path he basically considers
straight.

Although A. H. Bullen states that most of the play belongs to Middleton,[24] and Fredson Bowers agrees with Fleay's opinion that most of the play is Dekker's work,[25] both agree that Act V, scene 1, the most important scene in connection with this study, is Dekker's. It is a direct dramatization of Dekker's rogue pamphlets.

The scene is entirely devoted to Dekker's exposure of rogues. Moll and some of the more respectable characters are engaged in conversation when Trapdoor and Tearcat, his companion, appear, according to the stage direction, *"like a poore Souldier with a patch o're one eie, and* Tearcat *with him, all tatters."* Posing as a maimed soldier is one of the rogue's most common tricks, as *Belman* clearly demonstrates. Moll is at first ready to give them money—"by my troth I love a souldier with my soul." But after a careful perusal, she calls them "base rogues"—"Souldier? thou deserv'st to bee hang'd up by that tongue which dishonors so noble a profession, soldier you skeldering varlet?" Moll calls Tearcat a "whip-Jacke" and Trapdoor "an upright man"—both of these orders of rogue are described in *Belman.* She asks Tearcat if he is "a wild rogue, an angler, or a ruggler?"—more orders of rogue. This kind of dialogue goes on for one hundred lines, lines filled with cant terms and Peddlar's French. Moll explains many of the terms as she uses them, thereby serving as a living glossary of underworld jargon. She even challenges Trapdoor to cant with her. Moll and Tearcat sing a canting song—canting songs are found and translated in *Lanthorne and Candle-Light.* Dekker, in all of this, is presenting as much information as he can about the underworld; his audience was undoubtedly interested.

When Trapdoor and Tearcat leave, a cutpurse and his accomplices enter; Dekker must continue his exposé. These men represent a different part of the underworld, the city variety. The cutpurse is dressed "very gallant." He consults with his accomplices, wondering whether they should "shuffle in amongst yon heap of Gallants and strike." But Moll spoils their plans. She recognizes the cutpurse, "a diver with two fingers, a picke-pocket; all his traine study the figging law, that's to say, cutting of purses and foysting." She goes on to discuss the nip, snap, and stale, all described in *Belman*. Having been exposed—"smoakt," "Boyl'd"—the thieves leave. Moll then explains that she knows so much about thieves because she associated with them in her younger days. She has "seene their stings," she knows their laws. She admits that she has "a blacke ill name" because she knows "ill things," but she proclaims her knowledge to save Englishmen "from their quicke danger." This was Dekker's purpose in his rogue pamphlets. In short, a romanticized underworld character has become Dekker's spokesman in his exposure of the activities of the underworld. In his rogue pamphlets, no member of the underworld escaped Dekker's wrath; he played only upon the dark side of the underworld's image. In *The Roaring Girl* he causes the base string to vibrate to the merry antics of a girl in breeches, preferring, in the words of Middleton, "a slackeness of truth" to "fullnesse of slander."

The entire scene is packed with information which has no relation to the plot of the play, except that Moll once again plays the heroine. It is irrelevant and undramatic. Dekker and Middleton were obviously catering to the demands of an audience for whom exposés of the underworld had been of proven interest.

The Roaring Girl seems the logical product of Dekker's development, or change, during the period in which he deals with the seething life of his city. *The Honest Whore,* where a converted whore was forced to suffer for her past sins, was based on a traditional middle-class morality, shared by

Dekker and his audience. This morality was broken down in
the *Ho* plays, where the underworld as a satiric norm produced a new concept of the bourgeoisie. In *The Roaring Girl*
the very underworld that was forever distasteful and harmful
has as its main representative a romantic heroine whose main
function is to help a young man win his lady. The changes
in the presentation of Dekker's attitude toward the underworld
clearly indicate the corruption of a stern traditional moralist.
In the plays that follow this group, the underworld, although
less prominently displayed, continues to reveal Dekker's qualities of mind and art.

IV

In *If This Be Not a Good Play, The Devil Is In It* Dekker
works three separate plots which have no relation to one
another, except that a devil is found in each one. The play
begins in hell, where Charon complains to Pluto that his
boat business is bad and getting worse. As a remedy, Pluto
sends the devil Rufman to the court of the King of Naples,
Shacklesoule to a Friary, and Lurchall to become a merchant's
assistant. Each tries to get recruits to hell, but only Barterville,
the merchant, goes there. No underworld characters are
found in the play, except six courtesans who dance around
the Sub-Prior in the Shacklesoule plot. Yet, a Dekker play
dealing with hell must contain allusions to its related world
on earth. The relationship between the two underworlds appears within the first twenty lines of the play and continues
throughout. When Charon complains to Pluto that business
is bad he says:

> I fear th'infernall rivers are frozen or'e
> So few by water come: els the whores that dwell
> Next dore to hell, goe about.
>
> (I,1,14-16)

Charon maintains that in the good old days he had many
boat passengers because of the wars; however, times have
changed:

> But now these gallants which doe walke hells Rowndes,
> Are fuller of diseases, than of wounds.
> If wounded any take my boate, they roare,
> Being stabd, either drunke, or slaine about some whore.
>
> (I,1,37-40)

The audience's first glimpse of Rufman finds him "dancing a
bawde on's knee." Pluto, chastising his devils for laziness,
says:

> . . . were you honest divels
> Each officer in hell should have at least,
> A brace of whores to his break-fast: above us dwell,
> Divells braver and more subtile then in Hell.
>
> (I,1,74-77)

These references can be multiplied; the Devil-underworld relationship is strong—as it is in the rogue pamphlets and as it is
in the morality tradition. It helps to make hell more vivid
to the audience.

The six whores are introduced in the scene depicting the
Sub-Prior's temptation. He is the only virtuous man in the
monastery; his goodness and purity thwart Shacklesoule. The
Devil and his six courtesans dance around the Sub-Prior,
who shouts: "What sound offends mine eare? Soule of temptation? Enchanters I defie yee, get you gon." Hellish music
jars a pure man's ears. The whores leave saying: "Ha, ha, a
man of yce, a clod of clay." Candido too was a "man of yce"
in his relations with the underworld.

Barterville is the only character to go to hell because, as

Dekker makes clear, he is an oppressor, a cheater of his own class. His fraud and villainy alienate him from the citizen world; he preys upon his own class, like the underworld. He is corrupt without the help of the Devil. In fact he teaches the Devil a few tricks.

In this play the underworld, although of no importance in the play's structure, highlights the purity of one character, the Sub-Prior; throws a dark light on another character, Barterville; and gives hell an atmosphere of realism. It is used, therefore, exactly as it had been in the morality tradition and in Dekker's early plays. In *The Virgin Martyr,* however, the underworld once again becomes an important element in Dekker's dramaturgy.

The action of *The Virgin Martyr,* a collaboration between Dekker and Massinger, takes place in Rome at the time of the persecution of Christians. The worlds which are contrasted in this play, therefore, are the Pagan and the Christian. The external dichotomy between black and white shapes the morality of the dramatists. In the beginning of the play the characters are either good or evil; as the play progresses the Christian world absorbs many members of the Pagan world. Theophilus, assisted by the devil Harpax, is the main representative of the evil Pagan world. The final victory of the Christian world occurs when Theophilus turns Christian, frees the Christian slaves, and dies a martyr's death. The action proceeds along one direction, diverted by no subplots.

In the conflict between paganism and Christianity, the play's two underworld characters—Hircius, a whoremaster, and Spungius, a drunkard—both created by Dekker and both only in his scenes,[26] serve both worlds. They are the servants of Dorothea, who saved them from hanging, and later the henchmen of Harpax. But, significantly, even when they

serve Dorothea they are false to her; they are Pagans at
heart. In their first appearance they are complaining because
they have turned Christian. Hircius states:

When I was a Pagan, there was an Infidell Puncke of mine,
would have let me come upon trust for my corvetting, a pox
of your christian Coxatrices, they cry like Poulterers wives, no
money, no Cony.

(II,1,9-12)

Spungius also reminisces about the good old Pagan days.
After many complaints, they decide upon a remedy: to be
"halfe Pagans and halfe Christians." Spungius presents their
new attitude: "I am resolved to have an Infidels heart,
though in shew I carry a Christians face." They usually
preface their remarks with "As I am a Pagan," thereby forever indicating verbally their relation to the Pagan world.
Their anti-Christianity is clearly demonstrated when they relate that they are false to Dorothea. Spungius has used the
food sent by Dorothea to the poor for his own purpose—
"coynd the money into pottle pots of wine." Hircius was
given money to relieve and release prisoners, but he "took
common flesh for the money." Spungius is able to rationalize
Hircius' behavior: "And wisely done, for our Lady sending
it to prisoners, and bestowed it upon lowsie knaves, and thou
to save that labour casts it away upon rotten whores" (II,
1,70-72).

Angelo, the good spirit, knows that they are worthless. He
chastises them and tells them they are going "the divels way,
the way of sinne,/ The way of hot damnation, way of lust."
Later he emphasizes that "the divell waites on you." The
two, however, are incorrigibles. They betray Dorothea and
Antonio, the man who loves her but who is loved by the

Emperor's daughter. Dorothea is imprisoned; Hircius and Spungius have predictable plans for their reward: "I to my sweet placket." "And I to my full pot." Their money does not last long. They quarrel, calling one another thief and pickpocket. Angelo then gives them money to follow him to prison to bear part of Dorothea's sorrow. They accept the money, but desert him, with this rationalization:

HIRC: A way and shift for our selves, sheele do wel enough
        there, for prisoners are more hungry after mutton, then
        catch-poles after prisoners.
SPUN: Let her starve then if a whole Jayle will not fill her
        belly.

                                        (II,3,274-277)

This about the purest of women. At their next appearance the two are in rags and penniless. Spungius has spent his money in the tavern, Hircius has squandered his in the brothel —tavern and brothel, the traditional centers of sin in the morality tradition. Angelo meets them again and spurns them. Their rejection by the Christian world is complete. Angelo says, however, that he will pity them when they are sorry for their riots and when they tame their wild flesh "by labor." They express sorrow for their deeds, but the arrival of Harpax changes their attitude. The Devil can easily win over members of the underworld. Harpax tells them that the devil is "a wondrous good fellow, loves a cup of wine, a whore, any thing." The Devil is, therefore, like Hircius and Spungius. Harpax tells them that the Devil will give them anything when they are thoroughly acquainted with him—"call for a delicate whore; she's brought you. Be drunke as a beggar, he helps you home." They agree to torture Dorothea to win the Devil's favor. In Act IV Harpax gives them cudgels to beat Do-

rothea. They have some misgivings, but when he calls
them "silly Animals" (the underworld is a world of beasts)
and threatens them with punishment, they obey. They beat
Dorothea, but the blows do no damage. Theophilus, disgusted, beats them and orders that they be hanged. They
leave the stage guarded, and they are seen no more.

The two members of the underworld are, as traditionally
for Dekker and his audience, worthless and disgusting members of society.[27] Their basic filthiness of mind is reflected
in their attitude toward the pure Dorothea. They are part
of the Pagan world in action and sentiment. Judas-like they
betray the Virgin Martyr, who saved them from hanging.
They beat Dorothea with cudgels, but the pure cannot be
hurt by the underworld. They are dramatically associated
with the Devil, and therefore are strongly linked to the Pagan
world which has a close relationship to the Devil. Their future
home is hell. Whereas in *The Honest Whore* the citizen world
and the underworld clashed, in *The Virgin Martyr* the good
Christian world attempts to absorb the underworld, but is
betrayed for its efforts. Once Hircius and Spungius have betrayed Angelo, whose name is obviously significant, they can
no longer be forgiven. The underworld is thereby forcefully
thrown outside the pale of Christianity. Forgiveness of sin
was possible for a suffering Bellafront and for a thief on
the cross next to Christ; and forgiveness of sin was implied
in the easy conversion of Doll Hornet and in the superficial
repentances of rogue-pamphlet heroes. But in *The Virgin
Martyr* there is the strong implication that forgiveness of sin
is not universally possible. Dekker's presentation of Hircius and
Spungius, therefore, indicates not merely a reversion to the
strict moral pattern of *The Honest Whore* but an intensifica-
tion of that stern morality which is an essential, although easily
corrupted, part of his nature. *The Virgin Martyr,* being his

first non-comic play since *The Honest Whore,* has allowed Dekker to take a stronger and, in his case, more genuine moral stand. But more important, perhaps, than the genre of the play is the new collaborator whose moral position is close to his own. Massinger, unlike Webster and Middleton, presented his plays to instruct more than to entertain; he worked with characters who were either black or white; he was forever aware of the gravity of his moral purpose. Here indeed is a fitting associate for the Dekker of the rogue pamphlets and the Dekker who created a repentant Bellafront, a pure Candido and Sub-Prior, and a disgusting array of whores and bawds. Working with Massinger, Dekker not only avoided compromising his moral position, but even managed to make it stricter than tradition and his audience demanded.

In the tragicomedy *Match Me in London* Dekker, writing without a collaborator, once again deals with intrigue between court and citizens. However, it contains fewer citizens' wives and gallants than the *Ho* plays and *The Roaring Girl.* Here the intrigue concerns the King of Spain and Tormiella, the wife of the shopkeeper Cordolente. The only underworld figure in the play is the bawd, Dildoman, who has an important dramatic function. Dildoman supplies the lustful king with bed companions. She urges him to go to Cordolente's shop to look at the beautiful Tormiella. He does, and decides he must have her. Tormiella is secretly carried away from her husband's shop and lodged in the court, where Cordolente, disguised as a shoemaker, rushes to see his wife. The king, after many twists of plot and machinations in the court world, realizes that his lust has made him evil; he becomes reconciled with his queen. Tormiella and Cordolente are together again. All ends well—and the bawd will be punished.

Dekker effectively contrasts the court world and the citizen world. The king is presented as a lustful creature in sentiment, action, and his association with the bawd. He is the cause for the play's tragic overtones, since he is trying to ravish the pure wife of a citizen. Cordolente, like Candido, is a linen-draper and model of citizen virtue. He displays no fear, even when he ridicules the court at court. When the king makes Tormiella's father Vice-Admiral of the Navy, Cordolente states: "Oh spitefull Comedy, he's not a Courtier of halfe an houres standing, and he's made a Vice already" (IV,1,20-21). Tormiella, like Jane and the reformed Bella-front before her, is a model of virtue and is able to resist the bawd's temptations and the king's advances. Her spirit is typified by this comment to the king: "I will not be your whore to weare your Crowne./ Nor call any King my Husband, but mine owne" (III,3,93-94). The contrast be-tween the two worlds is comically epitomized in Act IV, scene 2, where Bilbo, Cordolente's journeyman, and a court Cox-comb exchange insults. Bilbo wins the match, of course. The underworld, represented by Dildoman, has the important func-tion of bringing the court and citizen worlds together. She brings the court world to the citizen world by showing the king Tormiella. This action brings the citizen world to court in the persons of Tormiella, Cordolente, and others. Essentially, the underworld acts as a bawd to the court and citizen worlds.

Dildoman, like all of Dekker's bawds, gets much abuse from the other characters. The king himself curses her, which gives the audience an indication that he is not completely evil.

> Th'art a damn'd Bawd:
> A soaking, sodden, splay-foot, ill-look'd Jade;
> Not all the wits of Kingdomes can enact
> To save what such Gulphes as thou art wrack'd,

Thou horie wickednesse, Divels dam, do'st thou thinke
Thy poysonous rotten breath shall blast our fame,
Or those furr'd gummes of thine gnaw a Kings name!
                              (II,2,92-98)

At the end of a play filled with scheming characters, she
is the only one to be punished. The king proclaims:

                              Let that slye Bawd,
            Engine of Hell, who wrought upon thy Chastity
            Be whipt through Sivill, foure such tempting witches
            May undoe a City.
                              (V,5,37-40)

In *Match Me in London* the citizens emerge triumphant
and completely clean. Dekker has reverted to the concept of
the bourgeoisie he held in *Shoemakers' Holiday* and *The
Honest Whore*. In the *Ho* plays the citizen-underworld association made the citizens coarse in the eyes of the audience.
Here Dekker attempts to isolate the citizens not only from
the underworld but from the court world as well, a new development for Dekker. He seems to desire a citizen class
free from all corruption, from above as well as below. Dildoman receives so much abuse and is the play's only punished
character because she is a member of the underworld *and*
because she wished to bring together the court and citizen
worlds, worlds which Dekker wants to keep apart. Although
Dekker's "voyce is decaying with my Age," as he states in
his dedication to Lodowick Carlell, it clearly shouts out for
an isolated pure citizen class and indicates the strict morality
that is essential Dekker.

The Witch of Edmonton—a collaboration between Dekker,
Ford, and Rowley—is at times a tragically powerful drama.
It contains no underworld characters, although Mother

Sawyer, who is accused of being a witch, is called a whore and is associated with the Devil. She acquires no other underworld characteristics, which can be considered a comment on the attitude of the dramatists toward her. They present her as a wretched old woman, harassed until she makes a pact with the Devil. Their treatment of her is, in the main, sympathetic. That she is often able to justify her own conduct is an indication that Dekker does not consider her a member of the underworld.

Dekker's last extant play, *The Wonder of a Kingdom,* is a conventional tragicomedy containing no underworld characters. Dekker, however, presents many allusions to the underworld, allusions which usually come from the mouth of the play's most unsympathetic character, Signior Torrenti. He is a riotous lord, who despises the poor, hates soldiers, and loves whores. Dekker, who loves the poor and soldiers and hates whores, uses the underworld in this play as it was used in the morality tradition: to indicate character. The man who says that harlots "shall feed me, fill me" must be punished in a Dekker play.

V

Dekker was a writer of the middle class for the middle class, and he viewed the underworld as the middle class would view it—with loathing *and* with interest. The underworld, as Chapter 1 has demonstrated, was a subject of interest for the Elizabethans. Dekker presents this world to his audience; he also abuses this world for his audience. He pleases their appetites by presenting low-life characters and realistic milieus, and at the same time he chastises the objects of their hatred and distrust.

Contemporary assumptions about the underworld shaped

Dekker's thinking. For Dekker and his London audience, the underworld was a world of filth and deceit. It was closely associated with the Devil's underworld. It was an enemy to society, especially to the citizen world. The members of the underworld were the foes of the government and the church. To the staunch Anglican Dekker they were a menace to everything that was clean and good. In the plays before 1604, although Dekker shows no dramatic interest in the underworld, his attitude toward the underworld is clear. With *The Honeset Whore* Dekker begins to represent the underworld on the boards. Some underworld character is found in most of his subsequent plays. His attitude toward the underworld—in pamphlet, allusion, or dramatic action—remains essentially the same from beginning to end of his career. Because his basic attitude is a constant, his treatment of the underworld becomes a revealing focus for understanding his quality as a dramatist, and serves, more than any other focus, to highlight his hack tendencies. His use of the underworld indicates when he does and does not work against his essential moral beliefs. In *The Honest Whore,* where his moral position is clearly translated into dramatic action, the underworld presents a strong contrast to the citizen world. In the *Ho* plays it easily meshes with the citizen world, thereby reversing the pattern of *The Honest Whore* and presenting a bourgeoisie that is now satirized. In *The Roaring Girl* the underworld is romanticized, breaking down even further the pattern of *The Honest Whore*. In *The Virgin Martyr,* however, the underworld is forcefully flung outside the bounds of Christian mercy, and in *Match Me in London* it is much abused for acting the bawd to the court and citizen worlds, with the citizen world once again glowing with virtue. There can be no doubt that Dekker has a sincere love for the citizen class, that the bourgeoisie represents for him the clean and good world—the world for which he writes and which dictates his morality. But there can also be no doubt that Dekker compromises his moral position whenever the external need arises. He can serve as the example *par excellence* of the strict traditional moralist corrupted by the pressures of theatrical compromise.[28]

Dekker's morality, when it is approached by way of the underworld, seems to influence his ability to construct a play. *The Shoemakers' Holiday* (where an underworld is absent; where the citizen world is filled with health and merriment) presents his most coherent plotting. *The Honest Whore* (where a converted harlot must suffer; where a Candido must avoid the underworld like the pox) is Dekker's most satisfyingly ordered play. *The Virgin Martyr,* drawing clear moral lines, is also well-ordered. *Westward Ho, Northward Ho,* and *The Roaring Girl* (where citizens' wives are comically wanton; where Doll Hornet is easily converted; where a cutpurse is glorified) display a looser morality and a much looser structure. When Dekker works against his basic moral beliefs he becomes an awkward craftsman; when he can draw clear moral lines, solidified by a love for the class which originally drew these lines, he presents aesthetically satisfying drama. For Dekker, a quality of mind seems to indicate a quality of dramaturgy. And the underworld provides the most revealing clue to understanding this mind.

4

Ben Jonson

In his Prologue to *Every Man Out of His Humour* Ben Jonson states that he will present a mirror in which the audience will see "the times deformitie/ Anatomiz'd in every nerve, and sinnew." Not nature, but the time's "deformitie." For Jonson's purpose in comedy was to castigate the follies of his time by holding them up to ridicule. His intention reveals him to be a conscious reformer and a realist. It is difficult to find an affectation, folly, or fraud of his day which is not reflected in Jonson's mirror. His work presents a picture of London which is vivid and varied. The underworld is an essential part of this picture. His treatment of and attitude toward the underworld clearly demonstrate his dramatic purpose and technique, and provide perhaps the most significant comment on the development of his art.

I

In the plays written before his great middle period (1606-1616) Jonson gives the underworld little attention. In these plays Jonson truly sports with follies, not with crimes, whereas in his mature period he is concerned with both. Here and there the underworld, in some form, appears in his early plays, but only to provide some realistic touches for local color. He has not as yet come upon a method to use the underworld as a structural entity or a moral reflector.

A constable, Tobie Turfe, is one of the main characters in *A Tale of a Tub,* probably Jonson's earliest play. The constable's daughter is sought by various suitors. One of them, John Clay, is falsely accused of being a robber, which causes Tobie to make Hue and Cry against him. But all of this is playful and part of the vogue of satire against constables. The play contains many references to thievery and Tyburn, also playful in the context of the love plot. The references merely give the play local color and help to make the comedy realistic, in the fashion of the early moralities.

Every Man in His Humour is Jonson's first important and successful play, because it presents vividly conceived characters playing their parts in a comedy of humours. Jonson reveals himself as a realist and a satirist at the writing of this play, eighteen years before he presents his clearest expression of his dramatic aim in the Prologue to the revised version of 1616.

> But deedes, and language, such as men doe use:
> And persons, such as *Comoedie* would chuse,
> When she would shew an Image of the times,
> And sport with humane follies, not with crimes.[1]

His humour characters, each dominated by a ruling passion or quirk, may seem caricatures to the modern reader; but to Jonson they were reflections of the creatures he observed around him—men who were vain, hypocritical, jealous, greedy, and ignorant. They are taken from the life around him, speak the language such as men do use, and are solidified in the world which he creates on stage. They play their roles against a background that testifies to Jonson's concern for realism. His comedies thereby become important social documents which give us a more accurate picture of Elizabethan life than the plays of either Dekker or Shakespeare.

His revision of the setting of *Every Man In* from Florence to London allows him to ridicule more effectively the English humours in an atmosphere familiar to his audience. Some of the characters in *Every Man In,* in addition to being humour characters, have names which carry a mildly allegorical significance, thereby connecting Jonson with the native tradition of the moralities, as does his didacticism. Another element of the moralities, which pertains to the underworld, also finds its way into this play—the tavern image. Knowell Senior reads the letter, sent by Wellbred to Edward Knowell, which indicates to him that his son is consorting with evil companions. The letter is sent from the Windmill Tavern, which causes Knowell Sr. to utter: "From the *Burdello,* it might come as well;/ The *Spittle:* or *Pict-hatch.*" Here Knowell Sr. associates the tavern with the stews, and feels that his son is being corrupted by vice. He resolves to bring his son back to virtue gradually. The tavern is operating here as it did in the moralities—as a corrupter of youth, with Wellbred as the evil angel and Knowell Sr. as the good angel.

The image appears again when Kitely complains to Downright that Wellbred is turning his house into a tavern.

He makes my house here common, as a *Mart,*
A *Theater,* a publike receptacle
For giddie humour, and diseased riot;
And here (as in a taverne, or a stewes)
He, and his wild associates, spend their houres,
In repetition of lascivious jests,
Sweare, leape, drinke, dance, and revell night by night,
Controll my servants: and indeed what not?
                              (II,1,61-68)

Kitely's opinion of Wellbred's carousing in his home is similar to Knowell Senior's appraisal of Wellbred and his son at the tavern. Knowell thinks that his son is in moral jeopardy, Kitely that his wife is. In both cases the underworld image is operating. And in both cases the image falsifies the truth, for neither Edward Knowell nor Kitely's wife is in danger. The image merely indicates the foolishness of both Knowell Sr. and Kitely. Later in his career, Jonson will replace the image with underworld characters for the similar function of ridiculing folly.

One other aspect of the underworld is found in the play. Brainworm's disguise as a disabled soldier is a typical rogue trick, familiar to the Elizabethans in the audience. But the disguise is one of many which Brainworm dons in order to help young Knowell; it gathers to itself none of the taint of the underworld. In fact, Jonson seems to betray an appreciation for the beggars who pose as war veterans. Whereas Dekker saw their rascality, Jonson delights in their ability to receive alms. He never loses this delight in intelligent trickery.

Although the names of the characters in *Every Man Out* are Italian, the play, like its predecessor, is a London play in which the follies of Englishmen are exposed. The characters are many, but not one is a member of the underworld. However, one character, Shift, is of some interest to this study because he feigns being a member of the underworld. In the preliminary character sketch Jonson says this about him: "He usurps upon cheats, quarrels, and robberies, which he never did, only to get him a name." Sogliardo, one of the objects of Jonson's satire, is completely taken in by Shift. He boasts about his friend to everyone.

SOGLIARDO:	. . . he has done five hundred robberies in his time, more or lesse, I assure you.
PUNTARVOLO:	What? and scapt?
SOGLIARDO:	Scapt! yfaith I: he has broken the jayle when he has been in yrons, and yrons; and beene out, and in againe: and out, and in; . . .
SHIFT:	Why 'tis nothing, sir, when a man gives his affections to it.

(IV,5,42-50)

When Shift is later accused of stealing Puntarvolo's dog because "he hath beene a notorious thiefe by his owne confession," Shift denies the theft. Hard pressed, Shift kneels and says: "Pardon me, good sir; god is my witnesse, I never did robberie in all my life." And then again: "I, (as I hope to be forgiven, sir) I ne're rob'd any man, I never stood by the high-way-side, sir, but only said so, because I would get my self a name, and be counted a tall man" (V,3,64-67). Sogliardo chases him from sight.

What is interesting here is that being a high member of the underworld, like a robber and highwayman, is prestigious. This attitude is part of the climate of opinion surrounding the underworld, as Chapter 1 has demonstrated. Sogliardo is a fool not because he considers a member of the underworld "a tall man," but because he is not a judge of character. In *Every Man Out* the underworld, in a small way, helps

Jonson point a satiric finger at one of his fools. It will be called upon far more brilliantly in his mature comedies.

The mythology of *Cynthia's Revels* allows for no underworld character. One reference to the underworld is of some interest, however. It comes from Crites, who refers to vice in this way:

> Tut, she is stale, ranke, foule, and were it not
> That those (that woo her) greet her with lockt eyes,
> (In spight of all the impostures, paintings, drugs,
> Which her bawd custome dawbes her cheekes withall)
> She would betray, her loth'd and leprous face,
> And fright th'enamor'd dotards from themselves.
>
> (I,5,49-54)

Vice is a whore, with Custom as the bawd who paints her cheeks. The image is a vivid one, presenting the conventional relationship between whore and painting which all dramatists of the age used. It suggests another aspect of the climate of opinion surrounding the underworld.

In the early part of his career, as in the last part, Jonson is an experimenter. He is never afraid to try something new, especially when it has its roots in something old. He drew many of his situations from Roman comedy, and in his presentation of character he often allies himself with the morality tradition. He saw himself as a realist with the important mission of ridiculing folly. In these early plays he makes no important use of the underworld in achieving this purpose. He presents not one underworld character and only a few uses of the underworld as idea, usually operating in the conventional climate of opinion. It is not difficult to see why. In his experiments he has not as yet seized upon his most effective method for satirizing the follies of Elizabethan society. Only when he realizes that he must deal with follies *and* with crimes, or, more specifically, follies by means of crimes, will he be able to give full scope to his dramatic and satiric powers. This he does in his mature period.

II

Jonson begins his mature period with *Volpone*. In the early period he sported with folly; now the word "sport" becomes too mild, for folly is often attacked severely. Before, folly pertained to mere eccentricity; now, the eccentricity is often a manifestation of a greed or hypocrisy that lies deep in the fool's personality. But, most important, beginning with *Volpone* Jonson uses the method which will carry his dramatic satire to its most effective results—the interaction between the cheated and the cheaters.

In *Volpone* Jonson turns to Venice for his scene and to the Italian institution of legacy-hunting for his device of bringing the cheated to the cheaters. It is the first play in which a character acts as a magnet to attract other characters. The source of attraction is Volpone, a rich Venetian who feigns sickness, and those attracted are his would-be heirs—Voltore, Corbaccio, and Corvino. Volpone, with the help of Mosca, plays upon the obsessive greed of the fools who seek his wealth and causes them not only to drain some of their own wealth in order to please him, but to behave unnaturally. For the love of money, Corbaccio is willing to disinherit his son, Corvino to prostitute his wife, and Voltore to distort and debase justice. The knaves, therefore, cause the fools to display not only their foolishness but their corrupt natures, in keeping with their beast names. Volpone displays his own kind of corruption and unnaturalness. Not only do his covetousness and lust emphasize his evil nature, but the physical presence of the eunuch, dwarf, and hermaphrodite become external symbols of his corruption. The game of cheater-cheated, therefore, is played by unnatural knave-fools in the stifling atmosphere of Venice, a city notorious as a seedbed of corruption. The world of Volpone is a closed, heavy, dark world, acting for Jonson as a microcosm of the real world which has its own varieties of unnatural fools and knaves.

Especially significant is the fact that Jonson in *Volpone* not only has discovered a structural device which will allow him to produce his greatest comedy by bringing a variety of fools to his knaves, but that he has also begun to play with the moral values of his audience. Volpone and Mosca are deceitful and covetous, but Jonson's most effective satire is directed against the fools. The audience may have little sympathy for the machinations of Volpone and Mosca, but it has absolute contempt for the greed and hypocrisy of Voltore, Corvino, and Corbaccio. Jonson displays two corrupt knaves who deceive three corrupt fools and one foolish Englishwoman, and challenges his audience to take sides. Choosing between two kinds of sin causes an audience to investigate its own values, and this is Jonson's particular aim. For example, what is more reprehensible—prostituting a wife for money or seducing a virtuous woman for pleasure? Volpone's encounter with Celia is especially enlightening in this connection. Celia is essentially a static colorless character, for whom the audience would feel no contempt and little sympathy. Volpone's attempted seduction is definitely the act of an irredeemably corrupt villain. It would seem that the audience's sympathy would be forced to lean toward Celia, but this is not the case.[2] Whether Jonson meant it or not—and critics are at odds on this point—there is something laughable about the rape scene. Either Jonson allowed the song to Celia to misdirect his intention of showing Celia's predicament or he purposefully desired his song to highlight the comedy of the situation. Judging from Jonson's method in his later plays of causing the audience to investigate its own moral position, the latter seems more plausible. The attempted rape causes one critic to talk of Volpone's "heroic vitality" in contrast to Celia's "anaemic virtue," [3] and another critic to refer to "Harpo Marx in pursuit of the too simply innocent female." [4] The audience, in short, is forced by Jonson to side with Volpone, as it will later be forced to side with an underworld which will also act as a seducer. Indeed, Volpone is like the Jonsonian underworld not only in his exposure of fools, but in the intelligence and virtuosity with which he conducts his knavery. These are the exact qualities which the Elizabethan audience has always respected.

This respect does not, however, lead Jonson to soften Volpone's punishment at the end of the play. Jonson, in *Volpone* as in his early plays, remains the stern satirist who doles out poetic justice—which he will not do in *The Alchemist* and *Bartholomew Fair*. Volpone is brought before Venetian judges; he will eventually acquire the sicknesses he had feigned. Mosca also suffers correction at the hands of justice and will be a perpetual prisoner. *Volpone,* therefore, essentially embodies the moral purposes that Jonson was forever proclaiming. Before the play is over every deviation from the moral norm is punished in one way or another. As Harry Levin asserts, "In *Volpone* he is still willing to sacrifice comedy to morality." [5] But within this moral framework Jonson has begun to play upon the moral assumptions of the audience and already indicates an attitude toward intelligent knavery that will achieve great importance in the plays dealing with the professional underworld.

When he turns to the writing of *The Alchemist* Jonson retains the structural device he has used so well in *Volpone* of having the deceived come to the deceivers. He changes the exotic atmosphere of Venice to the familiar atmosphere of London, retaining, however, some of the corruption—for his London is plague-ridden and the house in which the play takes place is closed and filled with fumes. The sinister victimizers of *Volpone* become members of the London underworld. Moral values become fuzzier; strict poetic justice is abandoned. And Jonson the judge becomes Jonson the observer.

Jonson's choice of the London underworld as his attractive center is both a happy and an important one. The reasons for the choice are many. It allows Jonson to exploit one of the chief elements in his art—the realistic presentation of London life. He seems happy to be on home ground again:

> Our *Scene* is *London,* 'cause we would make knowne,
> No contries mirth is better then our owne.

His use of the underworld permits him to present a rich variety of dupes from different social levels who could plausibly come to a specific place, the alchemist's laboratory, for a variety of reasons—thereby allowing Jonson to play upon the different motives and temperaments of the cheated. The underworld, by its very nature, was a dynamic center of attraction allowing the audience to become interested in the members of the underworld as characters. Contact between the underworld and its victims ensured the kind of heightened condition which produces effective drama and was of proven interest to an audience that devoured rogue pamphlets. Most important, and most revealing of Jonson's art, the underworld could serve as an effective instrument of cozenage at the same time that it provided the audience with a traditional moral bias. By playing underworld against fool Jonson heightens ironic perspective and forces his audience to investigate its own values.

In the play, Jonson capitalizes on the profession of alchemy, which had a vogue in Elizabethan England. It was a surefire and believable practice to draw together the cheaters and the cheated. The three rogues of the play—Subtle, Face, and Doll Common—are full-fledged members of the Elizabethan underworld. They have set up temporary headquarters in the house of Face's master, Lovewit, who has left London in order to escape contamination from the plague. The underworld forever thrives on disorder, and plague time provides the rogues with the perfect conditions for carrying on their cozening. In a sense, they become isolated from the world outside and can perform their illegal practices with a sense of security. This security will be destroyed when the atmosphere of the plague clears and the world outside knocks at the gates of the house. Before this happens, however, Jonson is able to use his rogues to exploit the folly, greed, and hypocrisy of the alchemist's clients, who provide an interesting cross section of London life—clerk, tobacco-man, knight, Puritan, "angry" country boy.

A vehement quarrel between Subtle and Face opens the play. The underworld not only spreads disorder, but is itself in a state of disorder. By means of their many accusations Jonson gives them a past. Each, according to the other, was in bad straits. Subtle, Face reveals, had picked his clothes out of dunghills. Face, according to Subtle, was himself taken out of dung. They shout epithets at one another—cheater, bawd, conjurer, cutpurse, witch. Face becomes so infuriated with Subtle that he threatens to "Write thee up bawd, in *Paules*." During the quarrel the role of the third partner in crime becomes evident. Doll forcefully puts an end to the strife, emphasizes the importance of the unholy alliance, and speaks of their cozening in loving terms:

Ha' you together cossen'd all this while,
And all the world, and shall it now be said
Yo'have made most courteous shift, to cosen your selves?

. . .

S'death, you perpetuall curres,
Fall to your couples againe, and cossen kindly,
And heartily, and lovingly, as you should,
And loose not the beginning of a *terme*,
Or, by this hand, I shall grow factious too,
And, take my part, and quit you.

(I,1,122-4;136-41)

Here, in the play's beginning, one aspect of Doll's importance
is accentuated. She keeps the two rogues together. Later
she will demonstrate that she is a competent cozener. Subtle
and Face recognize her worth; Face says:

. . . at supper, thou shalt sit in triumph,
And not be stil'd Doll Common, but Doll Proper,
Dol Singular: the longest cut, at night,
Shall draw thee for his Dol Particular.

(I,1,176-9)

Her importance to the rogues, therefore, rests not only on her
abilities as cony-catcher and pacifier, but also on her activities in bed. The sexual relationship between Subtle, Face,
and Doll, introduced so early in the play, suggests lust on
an elemental level, and will provide a point of comparison
with a later manifestation of lust.

Having presented the rogues and their relationship, Jonson
is now ready to introduce the first of his gulls, Dapper, a
lawyer's clerk. He is an obvious dupe for the clever Subtle
and Face. In fact, he reveals that he was robbed even before
he entered the rogues' den. Explaining why he is late, he
says: "And I had lent my watch last night, to one/ That

dines, to day, at the shrieffs: and so was rob'd/ Of my passe-time." He will be robbed of more than time before the play ends. He has come to acquire a familiar with which to win at horses, but before he leaves he is convinced that he is a favorite of the Queen of Faery, who will give him all her wealth. Gulling this fool is not difficult for Subtle and Face; rogues with less experience could have accomplished the task. Their next victim is Drugger, a tobacconist, whose desire is in keeping with his modest vocation; he wishes to know "by art" how to build his shop. Subtle, speaking in astrological and nonsensical terms, makes Drugger an easy dupe. The first two fools, therefore, allow the rogues to display some skill in cozening, but are no real challenge to their abilities because the clerk and tobacconist are obvious fools. Jonson points up their foolishness but treats them perfunctorily, because they are essentially "open" simpletons with modest and crude desires. He saves his most effective satire, and allows his rogues to display their great virtuosity in the art of cony-catching, when the excessively ambitious customers enter—Sir Epicure Mammon and the Puritans, Ananias and Tribulation Wholesome.

Sir Epicure Mammon, as Herford and Simpson believe, "stands apart and aloof" from the other dupes in the play.[6] He is a great voluptuary who desires nothing less than the philosopher's stone in order to acquire the riches for luxurious living. Mammon is the most enthusiastic of the gulls who come to Subtle; in heightened language he is forever dwelling on the luxuries he will possess and the desires he will gratify when the stone is his. Surly, his skeptical friend, attempts to dissuade him from his foolishness, but the epicurean is too steeped in the wonders of his imagination. The stone becomes the primary object of his lust, a lust which previously

has caused him to wish for wives and concubines equal with
Solomon's and the best paramours that money can buy. The
satire against Mammon becomes most effective when he
confronts Doll, who poses as a lord's sister and a scholar.
He tells her:

> There is a strange nobilitie, i' your eye,
> This lip, that chin! Me thinks you doe resemble
> One o' the *Austriack* princes.
>
> (IV,1,54-56)

The voluptuary who is so precise about his delicacies and
desires cannot tell a lady from a whore. He tells her of the
wonders of the philosopher's stone and what he will do for
her. His rich description, applied to a whore, heightens the
satire against him.

> . . . but come forth,
> And tast the aire of palaces; eate, drinke
> The toyles of Emp'ricks, and their boasted practise;
> Tincture of pearle, and corall, gold, and amber;
> Be seene at feasts, and triumphs; have it ask'd,
> What miracle shee is? set all eyes
> Of court a-fire, like aburning glasse,
> And worke 'hem into cinders; when the jewells
> Of twenty states adorn thee; and the light
> Strikes out the starres; that, when thy name is mention'd,
> Queenes may looke pale: and, we but shewing our love,
> Nero's Poppaea may be lost in storie!
>
> (IV,1,134-45)

The man who can address this speech to a whore, no matter
how effective her disguise, thrusts ridicule upon himself.
His lust for Doll recalls Volpone's lust for Celia. There the
audience sides with the knave; here it laughs at the fool.

Mammon's lust is shown to be absurd and rotten at the same time. The open, animal-like lust of Subtle and Face for Doll effectively contrasts with the orgy in Mammon's sick mind. The underworld, therefore, acts not only as an instrument of cozenage, but as a moral reflector.

Mammon's hopes will not be satisfied because his sinful lust, he is led to believe, has caused the alchemist's failure to produce the stone. This is the rogues' happiest stroke of villainous genius. Mammon's contact with the underworld has not only stripped him of his money, but has caused him to display his gullibility, his lust, and his avarice. He is the complete fool and the complete victim of the underworld, fit only to "preach/ The end o' the world."

Of all the dupes the greediest are the Puritans, Ananias and Tribulation Wholesome, who receive Jonson's greatest abuse. In its relations with Dapper, Drugger, and Kastril—the latter, desiring to become an angry boy, can be summarily dismissed as one of the more modest dupes—the underworld was merely an instrument of cozenage, showing these clients of the alchemist to be fools because they were tricked. With Mammon, the underworld not only tricked a fool, but served as a reflection of Mammon's depraved lust. With the Puritans, Jonson deepens his satire by making greater use of the underworld as a moral reflector. The Puritans desire the philosopher's stone in order to raise the fortunes of the holy brethren of Amsterdam and convert the world. The zealous Ananias enters in II,5, and Jonson's satire on the Puritans begins immediately. When Subtle asks him, "Who are you?" Ananias answers, "A *faithfull Brother,* if it please you." To which Subtle replies:

> What's that?
> A *Lullianist?* a *Ripley? Filius artis?*

Can you *sublime,* and *dulcefie? calcine?*
Know you the *sapor pontick? sapor stiptick?*
Or, what is *homogene,* or *heterogene?*
(II,5,7-11)

Subtle pretends to believe that Ananias is a fellow professor
of Alchemy. The alliance between Puritan and alchemist begins with this verbal quibble and grows throughout the play—
indicating the overlapping between two kinds of chicanery.
Ananias tells Subtle that the Brethren refuse to give him
any more money until results are produced. Subtle, knowing
exactly how to treat his victims, drives him out of the house.
In III,2, as Subtle expected, Ananias returns with his elder,
Tribulation Wholesome. The scene points up the greed and
hypocrisy of the Puritans. They hope to increase the wealth
and prestige of the brotherhood by means of the philosopher's
stone, and Subtle plays upon this hope. Tribulation even
wonders whether "We may be temporall lords, our selves."
Ananias periodically interrupts the speeches of Subtle to present petty pieces of piety—"Bells are prophane." "It is,
indeed, an idoll" (referring to the Starch that women put
in their linens). "Christ-tide, not Christ-masse." His zealous
concern for these petty matters accentuates his unconcern
for the grosser sins that Subtle relates.

Subtle tells the Puritans that with the stone they will not
have to "raile against playes" or "lie with zealous rage,
till you are hoarse." And:

Nor call yourselves
By names of Tribulation, Persecution,
Restraint, Long-Patience, and such like, affected
By the whole family, or wood of you,
Onely for glorie, and to catch the eare
Of the *Disciple.*

Tribulation does not contradict Subtle's remarks:

> Truely, sir, they are
> Wayes, that the *godly Brethren* have invented,
> For propagation of the glorious cause,
> As very notable meanes, and whereby, also,
> Themselves grow soone, and profitably famous.

Tribulation agrees with Subtle that the names are invented—
for the propagation of a cause. The various names that Subtle
uses in connection with his alchemy are also invented for a
cause. Once again, the Puritan and the Alchemist seem very
similar.

Jonson, by means of the contact between underworld and
Puritans, is able to demonstrate that greed motivates both
cheater and cheated. He also equates them by his use of
language, for both Subtle and the Puritans have professional
jargons. Because Jonson contrives his stage speech so effectively, the audience feels that both jargons are the products
of falsely subtle minds. In accentuating the alliance between
the Puritans and the underworld, and by counterpointing
their jargon, Jonson forces the audience to transfer to the
Puritans some of the baser opinions it holds toward the
underworld; at the same time, he allows the underworld to
retain the respect of the audience because of its superior
intelligence in deceiving the Puritans. Jonson is fully exploiting the traditional ambiguity toward the underworld and
twisting it to his purpose. His satire against the Puritans
is so effective that one leaves the play thinking that the Puritans are greedy, petty, and hypocritical—and inferior to the
very underworld which has, for the most part, been reflecting
their position.

The return of Lovewit puts an end to the activities of
Subtle, Face, and Doll. The rogues, having operated in the

security of a house isolated from the world outside, now must reckon with that world. But the reckoning is a mild one, coming for Subtle and Doll in the person of their colleague Face, and coming for Face in the person of his master Lovewit. The rogues fall out, as the quarreling in the play's beginning foreshadowed. Subtle and Doll decide to trick Face and keep all their loot. Subtle justifies their intended deceit with this remark:

> To deceive him
> Is no deceipt, but justice, that would breake
> Such an inextricable tye as ours was.
>
> (V,4,102-4)

It is an important remark because it points to the idea of justice that is operating in the special, contained world in which the rogues perform their acts of thievery. To the underworld, and to Jonson who uses his underworld as an instrument of cozenage, there is justice in deception. Once the three rogues have performed justice in deceiving the dupes, it is left for one of the rogues, Face, to perform justice on the other two. It is fitting that he should do so, because he has proven himself to be the rogue with the greatest intelligence and the quickest wit. Having revealed all to Lovewit, Face—now Jeremy the butler—has the situation completely in hand. He causes his two accomplices to leave empty-handed, but not before he mocks them.

> All I can doe
> Is to helpe you over the wall, o' the back-side;
> Or lend you a sheet, to save your velvet gowne, Dol.

> Dol, I am sorry for thee i-faith. But hearst thou?
> It shall goe hard, but I will place thee some-where:

> Thou shalt ha' my letter to mistris Amo.
> . . . Or madame Caesarean.

> Subtle,
> Let's know where you set up next; I'll send you
> A customer, now and then, for old acquaintance.
>   (V,4,132-34;139-42;144-45)

The cozeners do not escape abuse completely; they are mocked and leave somewhat ignominiously—but free. Jonson chose the best instrument for mocking the rogues, another rogue. At the end of the play Face turns to the audience and says:

> Gentlemen,
> My part a little fell in this last *Scene,*
> Yet 'twas *decorum.* And though I am cleane
> Got off, from Subtle, Surly, Mammon, Dol,
> Hot Ananias, Dapper, Drugger, all
> With whom I traded; yet I put my selfe
> On you, that are my countrey: and this pelfe,
> Which I have got, of you doe quit me, rests
> To feast you often, and invite new ghests.
>   (V,5,157-65)

He is asking for public approval of his cozenage and he received it by the audience's applause. And the audience must applaud his cleverness and skill, as it had mentally applauded the cleverness and skill of many a rogue in pamphlet, song, and real life. The poetic justice operating in the play, therefore, is based on appreciation of his wit, which helps to explain why the underworld goes unpunished. Even though the outside moral world, knocking at the gate, seeks retribution, Jonson still allows the possessors of wit to triumph. A man called Lovewit will by his very nature side with the Faces of the world, be they rogues or no. His return does not produce an impartial judge who will dispense strict justice. He, in fact, reaps the fruits of the rogues' activities. The justice performed in the play is the only kind of justice possible in the world of rogues and fools which Jonson has created. It is not that Jonson's rogues are extremely likable; one is not dealing here with Falstaff or Charlie Chaplin. Doll Common is not the whore with the heart of gold of the modern theater. Nor are Subtle and Face romanticized. Yet, even realistically treated, the underworld, when compared *only* to fools, becomes the world to which the audience is committed. By providing an ironic perspective, Jonson beguiles the audience into siding with intelligent rogues against folly and hypocrisy. He does not include the underworld in his moral judgment, because in the world of comedy which he creates such a judgment would be superfluous, and because in the self-contained world of the play justice depends on intelligence. His satire falls on the cozened, not the cozeners, who become the dispensers of justice in the play. Jonson is more interested in ridiculing folly than crime. His satire is operating in a context less moral than in *Volpone* or the plays of the early period. At the same time, it is operating in an atmosphere more genial and more truly comic.

In *Bartholomew Fair* Jonson creates an underworld that is his most dynamic center of attraction. It operates in the open holiday atmosphere of Smithfield, not in the stifling air of dark Venice, or the closed fumy house in a plague-ridden London. Yet, as in *Volpone* and *The Alchemist,* it is a self-contained world which will act as an instrument of satire against those from the outside who approach it. At the Fair each member of an assorted crew of underworld figures carries on his or her particular trade for the purpose of making money. To the Fair come different grades of London citizenry. The contact between the underworld and the citizens produces not only Jonson's most effective satire and most genial laughter, but a sympathy for low humanity that Jonson has never displayed before or since.

The underworld of the Fair is seen for the first time in Act II. Before this act, Jonson introduces the various characters who are going to the Fair, all of whom will be affected, in a major or a minor way, by the Fair. Some will be gulled, some will be chastised, some will find fortune, some will be enlightened. Their characters are revealed even before they come into contact with the underworld, but the underworld provides the heightened conditions which will accentuate their follies and hypocrisies.

The play's most obvious gull is Bartholomew Cokes. He is young, loose-brained, naïve, and stupid. His visit to the Littlewits in Act I typifies him as the country gull. His misunderstanding of the words and sentiments of his bride-to-be, Grace Wellborn, points up his stupidity, as does his tutor's opinion of him. The seriousness and surliness of Waspe accentuate his pupil's flightiness. Even before his visit to the Fair, Cokes is recognized as the obvious victim for any kind of chicanery. Waspe, because of his surliness, self-righteousness, and dislike of pleasure, also shows himself to be a prospective object for satire. He dislikes the Fair for personal reasons. Those who dislike it for public reasons, Zeal-of-the-Land Busy and Justice Adam Overdo, become even greater objects of scorn. The Puritan Busy immediately reveals his hypocrisy by allowing the Littlewits and Dame Purecraft, whom he wishes to marry, to go, in his company, to the Fair, despite the fact that the Puritans objected to this practice. His fondness for eating influences his decision: roast pig may be eaten *if* "it be eaten with a reformed mouth,

with *sobriety,* and humbleness." His words indicate his
hypocrisy. Justice Overdo will go to the Fair in disguise in
order to discover enormities. He reveals an essential foolishness and pettiness when he wishes that all men in authority
would follow the example of that man who went to alehouses
to measure the length of puddings and weigh the loaves of
bread in order to discover corruption. His words turn against
him when he says:

They have seene many a foole in the habite of a Justice; but
never till now, a Justice in the habite of a foole. Thus must we
doe, though, that wake for the publike good: and thus hath the
wise Magistrate done in all ages.

(II,1,7-11)

He is resolved to "make mine owne discoveries" at the Fair—
"in Justice name, and the King's; and for the Commonwealth," an expression, repeated by him throughout the play,
which points up his pomposity. Overdo does tend to strike
terror in the underworld, but E. A. Horsman puts Overdo
in proper perspective by stating that he is "after all only a
Justice of the Peace, an inferior magistrate, presiding over
the lowest, if the most expeditious, court in the kingdom, the
Pie-powders, and even there only as representative of the
Lord of the Fair." [7]

Act II, scene 2 plunges the audience into the robust atmosphere of the Fair itself. Immediately, a quarrel is witnessed
between Leatherhead and Joan Trash, the first of many
quarrels within the Fair's underworld. As in *The Alchemist,*
the underworld is a world of disorder, but also as in *The
Alchemist,* the members of the underworld unite to cheat those
who will provide them with a livelihood. The Falstaffian
Ursula berates her tapster Mooncalf, at the same time that

she tells him how to water the ale—advice that reminds one of the antics of an early underworld character, the alewife of the miracle plays. She curses the horse-courser Knockem, but later asks for his help in transforming Win Littlewit into a whore. The quarrels pervade the chaotic Fair, but they do not interfere with the underworld's ability to carry on the business of cheating and stealing.

In its relations with Cokes, the underworld is merely an instrument of cozenage, like the underworld of the cony-catching pamphlets. Jonson here draws on traditional material to dramatize the antics of the cheaters preying upon an obvious dupe. The cutpurse, the hero of many a rogue pamphlet, here presents an heroic figure in the person of Ezekial Edgworth. Ezekial first picks the purse of Cokes when Overdo draws a crowd, attentive to his lecture on the evils of tobacco and ale. Cokes, his spirits difficult to dampen, puts another purse where the first was, openly challenging the crowd's anonymous pickpurse, who again strikes, while Cokes is happily listening to Nightingale's ballad about a youth who was hanged for cutting a purse. The gull is abused for a third time when he stoops to pick up the fallen fruit of the Costermonger, an accomplice in crime of Edgworth. Now that his hat, sword, cloak, and purses have been stolen, he correctly evaluates the goings-on at the Fair.

Would I might lose my doublet, and hose, too; as I am an honest man, and never stirre, if I thinke there be any thing, but thieving, and cooz'ning, i' this whole *Fayre*.

(IV,2,68-70)

However, the audience can be sure that this evaluation will not stop him from remaining a gull. Excited about the puppet show, he states: "I am in love with *Actors* already, and I'll be allyed to them presently." Cokes, in his contact with the underworld, has already demonstrated that he, in his brainlessness, is "allyed" to the puppets he loves. To point up his foolishness Jonson merely allows the underworld to act upon him, as upon Dapper and Drugger in *The Alchemist,* in the most obvious way. The obvious gulling of Cokes, however, allows Jonson to extend his satire. For Cokes is cozened when morality is most explicit. Overdo's speech and Nightingale's ballad on the cutpurse provide the underworld with the proper conditions for cozening. Morality, therefore, becomes the agent of the underworld. Jonson, in satirizing a fool, manages at the same time to satirize cheap and empty moralizing.

Waspe too is acted upon directly. Edgworth steals the box containing the marriage license which Waspe took from Cokes so that it would not be stolen. But Jonson's ridicule of Waspe is based not on the fact that an obvious fool was gulled, as with Cokes, but that a self-righteous busybody was gulled. The theft illuminates the fallibility of a man who thinks he cannot be deceived. He is, in the words of Quarlous, a "serious ass," which to Jonson seems to be worse than a happy ass, like Cokes. Waspe is too prone to chastise any kind of pleasure-seeking. The violence of his initial reaction to Coke's desire to go to the fair—"Bless me! deliver me, help, hold me! the Fair!"—indicates not only his concern for what the Fair could do to his charge, but also his basic aversion to cakes and ale. In waspishly hating everything and everybody, he seems to reduce life to the excrement that is forever a part of his speech. The underworld helps to expose him to others and to himself. For only after being placed in the stocks and learning that Cokes has knowledge of this clear disgrace is Waspe able to say: "He that will correct another, must want fault in himself." Waspe, like the play's other would-be reformers, Busy and Overdo, is guilty of self-deception, but whereas Waspe wishes to reform his foolish charge, Busy and Overdo wish to reform nothing less than Man.

Zeal-of-the-Land Busy is forever evaluating the Fair: "the place is *Smithfield,* of the field of Smiths, the Grove of Hobbi-horses and trinkets, the wares are the wares of divels. And the whole *Fayre* is the shop of Satan." After he has fully gorged himself with Ursula's roast pig his chastisement of the shop of Satan forcefully begins. He rails against long hair, tobacco, and ale; he condemns Leatherhead's toys and Joan Trash's gingerbread men—the former are idols, the latter images in a "basket of Popery." He presents this piece of invective against Ursula:

But the Fleshly woman (which you call Ursla) is above all to be avoyded, having the marks upon her, of the three enemies of Man, the World, as being in the *Faire;* the Devill, as being in the fire; and the Flesh, as being her selfe.

(III,6,33-37)

Knockem correctly characterizes Brother Busy by saying, "An excellent right Hypocrite! now his belly is full, he falls a railing and kicking, the Jade." Busy's excessive zeal causes so much commotion that he is carried off to the stocks, where he continues to preach. He is now a martyr to the "holy cause." When he is put in the stocks, he says that he "rejoiceth in his affliction, and sitteth here to prophesie the destruction of *Fayres* and *May-games, Wakes,* and *Whitsonales,* and doth sigh and groane for the reformation, of these abuses" (IV,6, 89-92). Having been delivered from the stocks "by a mir-acle," he rushes to denounce the puppet play, like his Eliza-bethan counterparts. He agrees to dispute with one of the puppets, and is effectively confounded when the puppet, by lifting up its garment, proves that there are neither males nor

females among them. Busy says: "I am confuted, the *Cause*
has failed me." The bumbling, over-zealous, wordy moralist is
beaten in argument by a wooden figure. To present the
appalling hypocrisy of the Puritan, Jonson uses his underworld not primarily as an instrument of cozenage, although
Busy is put in the stocks because of the underworld's machinations, but as the recipient of abuse. It is not necessary for the
underworld to act upon Busy; it merely has to be itself. For
the underworld acts as a spur to Busy's repetitious sermoniz-
ing, thereby exposing his narrow mind. He condemns what
he does not understand. His verbal clash with the underworld
fully reveals him to the audience.

Justice Overdo attempts to judge and destroy what he
does not even recognize. His first contact with the Fair indicates his inability to dwell on anything but trivialities, which
he considers enormities. When Leatherhead threatens to reveal
what Joan's gingerbread is made of—"stale bread, rotten eggs,
musty ginger, and dead honey"—the disguised Overdo, over·
hearing the argument, says: "I! have I met with enormity, so
soone?" In his first meeting with the Fair's "Bartholomew
birds" he applies the word "enormity" to something as inconsequential as the ingredients of gingerbread. He incor-
rectly observes what is around him. He decides to give assistance to a "civil young man," who happens to be the
cutpurse Edgworth.

What pitty 'tis, so civill a young man should haunt this debaucht
company? here's the bane of the youth of our time apparent.
A proper penman, I see't in his countenance, he has a good
Clerks looke with him, and I warrant him a quicke hand.

(II,4,30-34)

A quick hand he has. Overdo, like many objects of Jonson's
scorn, completely misjudges character. For not only is his

young man a cutpurse; he is as "debaucht" as the company
he keeps. It is Ezekial who is looking forward to the
"smockes," the "good whimsies," that the Bawd Whit will
provide for the night's entertainment. Overdo resolves that
he must rescue the youth. While preaching against the dangers
of tobacco and ale, his words draw a crowd that enables
Edgworth to cut Cokes's purse and display how quick his
hand is. Even when beaten by Waspe as the accomplice of
the cutpurse, Overdo will not discover who he is, "come
beating, come imprisonment, come infamy, come banishment,
nay, come the rack, come the hurdle." He will be a martyr
to the cause of justice. He will continue his efforts to rescue "this proper young man," Edgworth, "from his debaucht
company." His martyrdom becomes complete when he is
thrown into the stocks, again because he is mistaken for an
accomplice of the cutpurse. A justice of the peace, therefore,
in his contact with an underworld he cannot even discover,
is mistaken for a member of, and suffers the punishment
reserved for, that underworld. But his predicament only
causes him, as it caused Busy, to enjoy his martyrdom.

The world will have a pretty tast by this, how I can beare adversity: and it will beget a kind of reverence, toward me, here-
after, even from mine enemies, when they shall see I carry my
calamity nobly, and that it doth neither breake mee, nor bend
mee.

(IV,1,29-33)

When he escapes from the stocks, he, again like Busy, di-
rects his attention to the puppet show, where he theatrically
doffs his disguise, reveals himself, and begins to expose his
enormities—"looke upon mee, O *London!* and see mee, O
Smithfield; the *example of Justice,* and *Mirror of Magistrates:*
the true top of formality, and scourge of enormity." (V,5,

33-36). One of these enormities is his own wife, masked, whom he calls "my greene Madame." Quarlous exposes Overdo's folly by informing him that "your *Innocent young man,* you have tane such care of, all this day, is a *Cutpurse;* that hath got all your brother Cokes his things, and help'd you to your beating, and the stocks." He tells Overdo to "remember you are but *Adam,* Flesh and blood! you have your frailty, forget your other name of *Overdoo,* you invite us all to supper." Overdo, perhaps a changed man, does invite everyone to supper—"for my intents are Ad correctionem, non ad destructionem; Ad aedificandum, non ad dirvendum."

Overdo's contact with the underworld illuminates his own ineffectuality and misguided fervor. He cannot, in the words of Ray Heffner, "differentiate between the minor vanities and major iniquities of the fair." [8] The Fair is saturated with members of the underworld, but he can apprehend none. Apprehension must be based on comprehension. Only fools cannot comprehend the true nature of the Fair—which, as John Enck asserts, "is as obvious as the philosophers' stone was elusive" [9]—and therein rests Jonson's greatest indictment not only of Overdo, but Busy and Cokes and, to a lesser extent, Waspe.

The scene in which Jonson brings together his three moralists in the stocks presents a visually scathing indictment of reform based on ignorance. In it Jonson achieves an effective irony, for the very reformers who would put the underworld in the stocks find themselves there instead. Their punishment highlights their ineffectuality. Waspe, recognizing his disgrace, escapes by slipping his hand in the stocks instead of his foot. Busy, supposedly happy to be separated from the "heathen of the land," and Overdo, a "stoic in the stocks," gladly escape when the mad Troubleall causes confusion. Jonson uses the stocks, an instrument designed to chasten a disorderly underworld, to indicate visually the absurdity of the reformers' "position," and to suggest, with Troubleall's question ringing in the air, that the moralists have no warrant for attempting to correct what they cannot understand.

In his ridicule of the misdirected preacher and magistrate, Jonson uses the underworld as a catalyst. It brings out the fool in Busy and Overdo without itself significantly acting upon them or changing because of them. In serving as a catalyst it gathers to itself greater importance than the underworld ever attained in Jonson's work. For in *Bartholomew Fair* the underworld not only provides an ironic perspective as in *The Alchemist*—in a world of rogues and fools, is it better to be a rogue?—but also embodies the old Adam, flesh and blood, which the moralists of the play do not see in others or themselves. The animal-like qualities of the underworld, which condemn the underworld in the traditional climate of opinion and which is used by Dekker to criticize the underworld, is transformed by Jonson, in this play, into the animal energies and appetites of which all men partake. When all men partake, who can condemn? Looking for a jordan is not a normal pursuit in drama, but Jonson uses it to suggest that in some essential matters the citizens' wives and Poor Alices of the world are one. When Dekker brought together the whores with the citizenry in the *Ho* plays, he was aiming at mild satire of the citizens. Jonson goes much deeper, for he is emphasizing that the recognition that we are all but Adams is the only basis for a morality that avoids the self-righteousness of a Busy and an Overdo. In the world of *Bartholomew Fair* the underworld becomes emblematic of essential Man.

At the same time, the Fair mirrors society. The preying and whoring at the Fair is a reflection of the preying and whoring outside it. When the outside world enters the Fair's atmosphere, truth is revealed. In proposing to the disguised Quarlous, Dame Purecraft tells of her own kind of cozening and Busy's:

These seven yeeres, I have beene a wilfull holy widdow, onely to draw feasts, and gifts from my intangled suitors: I am also by office, an assisting *sister* of the *Deacons,* and a devourer, in stead of a distributor of the alms. . . . Our elder, *Zeale-of-the-land,* would have had me, but I know him to be the capitall Knave of the land, making himself rich, by being made *Feoffee* in trust to deceased *Brethren,* and coozning their *heyres,* by swearing the absolute gift of their inheritance.

(V,2,53-56;66-70)

Win, finding herself in Ursula's booth, displays a virtue that is frail. She is easily persuaded by Whit and Knockem that she can lie with twenty men and "be honest still." She even puts on the green gown of the whore. Her virtue, however, remains intact, as does the virtue of Mistress Overdo, who is taken for a high-class whore by Ramping Alice, the punk of Turnbull, and who also dons green. Quarlous, who vigorously chastises Edgworth for offering him a whore and who asserts that he is not one of Edgworth's "companions in beastlinesse," does not inform against the cutpurse, whose performance he witnessed, and even hires him to do a job. ("We are no catchpoles nor constables.")

The members of the outside world become absorbed in the atmosphere of the underworld and reveal their kinship to it. Mistress Overdo and Win are incipient whores. Quarlous and Winwife hire a cutpurse to do their stealing for them. Overdo is mistaken for a cutpurse's accomplice. Dame Purecraft and Busy are cozeners. Overdo, Busy, and Waspe receive the punishment of the underworld by being placed in

the stocks. At the Fair flesh and blood make the whole world
kin. Even Cupid, in the puppet show, becomes a pimp to
that whore Hero.

That the Fair is a symbol of the world is evident from the
play's beginning.[10] In the Induction, toward the end of the
Scrivener's speech, these words appear:

And though the *Fayre* be not kept in the same Region, that
some here, perhaps, would have it, yet thinke, that therein the
Author hath observ'd a speciall *Decorum,* the place being as
durty as *Smithfield,* and as striking every whit.

(156-161)

The audience has more than a suggestion here that the
Fair on stage represents not only the Bartholomew Fair of
Smithfield—where rogues carry on their vocations amidst
dirt and stench—but also the world itself. Nightingale's ballad on the cutpurse is especially interesting in this connection.
The meaning of a traditional moralistic ballad condemning
a common Elizabethan thief is extended by Jonson to include
a world of thieves. The individual condemnation becomes
general in the closing verses of the ballad:

> But O, you vile nation of cutpurses all,
> Relent and repent, and amend and be sound,
> And know that you ought not, by honest mens fall,
> Advance your owne fortunes, to die above ground,
> > And though you goe gay,
> > In silkes as you may,
> It is not the high way to heaven (as they say).
> > (III,5,146-152)

Edgworth cuts Cokes's purse at the very moment that Nightingale sings these words. Surely, Jonson is allowing a specific

act of thievery to acquire a broad symbolic meaning, for at the microcosmic Fair life does cut one's purse and fools will be caught unawares.

The underworld of *Bartholomew Fair,* therefore, becomes Jonson's richest satiric weapon. It acts not only as an instrument of cozenage, but is also a moral reflector and rich symbol. The members of the underworld receive no moral condemnation from Jonson—indeed, those who attempt to indict them *in the play* are ridiculed. In *The Alchemist* Jonson had allowed Subtle and Doll Common to go free and Face to reap some rewards. They were clever rogues and could be respected for their wit. But they were never as likeable as the Fair's rogues. Ursula and those who cheat around her are infused with a humanity that is in keeping with their symbolic function. Jonson fully responds to their human qualities; they are flesh and blood. He gives them a definite charm, without sacrificing his realism. Even their language, as Jonas Barish points out,[11] which continuously assaults the ear, carries no moral stigma. They are dirty, sordid cheaters operating in an atmosphere smelling of pig and punk. But they have a quality which the outsiders do not have—self-knowledge. They appear what they are, and they accept themselves for what they are. The would-be reformers cannot accept them for what they are; cannot, that is, discover the underworld's true nature, and are therefore ridiculed. Since part of the underworld's true nature is Everyman's, the fools display an ignorance of themselves, which is, to Jonson's mind, the greatest "disease of the *Soule.*"[12] Jonson has once again allowed his audience neither to condemn nor condone his underworld, while he has forced his audience to laugh at the underworld's prey, especially at the would-be reformers who can come to terms with Ursula's roast pig, but not with Ursula who, in her very fleshiness, represents a world that must be understood before it is condemned, if it is to be condemned at all. The happiest combination of Jonson's talents as a realist and a satirist is found in a play which fully exploits the underworld as a vital center of attraction, an instrument of cozenage, a moral reflector, and a symbol. Jonson would never again be so genial an observer of the human scene, nor would his laughter ever so effectively mock the human condition.

III

Although written a short two years after *Bartholomew Fair* and a long nine years before the first play of his late period, *The Staple of News, The Devil is an Ass* can be considered the beginning of Jonson's decline as a dramatist. The material that produced his great comedies—the relationship between fool and cheater—is found in this play, but it is not informed by the same technique or spirit. Previously, the cheaters had been the attractive center drawing the fools to them; now, the fool is the center. Previously, the cheaters were treated with some respect for their intelligence and in *Bartholomew Fair* with some warmth because of their humanity; now, Jonson's scorn envelops both cheater and fool. Previously, comedy was more important than morality; now, comedy seems secondary to it.

In *The Devil is an Ass* Jonson, like Dekker in *If This Be Not a Good Play, the Devil Is In It,* employs not one underworld, but two—the underworld of London and the underworld of Hell. Both underworlds are attracted to the play's center, Fabian Fitzdottrel, a wealthy vain fool. The play opens in the underworld of hell, where Satan attempts to dissuade Pug from venturing into London, because he is too ineffectual a devil. Satan declares that "The state of Hell

must care/ Whom it imployes, in point of reputation,/
Heere about *London*" (I,1,29-31). Pug desires to prove his
worth, and is given permission to go to London for a day.
He would like a Vice to accompany him. Old Iniquity appears and recites his many tricks of old. He promises to bring
Pug to bawds and whores for wenching and to taverns for
drinking. He wishes, in short, to acquaint the devil Pug, as he
acquainted the Everyman of the moralities, with the world of
sin. Satan rejects Iniquity; he would be completely useless on
earth now, in modern times. Jonson's London requires a
"Vice of quality," not Old Iniquity. The play's opening
scene, therefore, not only presents a delightful parody on the
plays in the morality tradition, but indicates the inadequacy
of the morality of that tradition in the Jacobean age.

The underworld of hell and the underworld of London
become one when Pug takes the body of "a handsome Cutpurse hang'd at Tiborne." With this body he must serve
Fitzdottrel, whose great desire is to be served by the devil
in order to gain more wealth and social prestige. Fitzdottrel
does get a devil for a servant, but does not realize this. In
order to gain wealth and prestige, therefore, he turns to Meercraft, a London swindler who would have been the play's
center had Jonson followed the technique of his previous plays.
Meercraft is a projector, which is defined by Engine.

> Why, one Sir, that projects
> Wayes to enrich men, or to make 'hem great,
> By suites, by marriages, by undertakings:
> According as he sees they humour it.
>   (I,7,10-13)

Whereas Subtle promised to enrich men by means of alchemy, Meercraft relies on the various schemes and projects
that his shrewd mind can invent. These range from the re-

covery of all submerged land in England to a monopoly on toothpicks. Although he promises less than the philosophers' stone, his suggested patents and monopolies play upon the avaricious minds of a number of fools. Fitzdottrel is his most foolish victim. His first words in the play are: "Sir, money's a whore, a bawd, a drudge;/ Fit to runne out on errands: Let her goe." That is exactly what he persuades the gull Fitzdottrel to do—let money go. Fitzdottrel is the willing dupe of every Meercraft scheme, culminating in Fitzdottrel's pose as the victim of possession by the devil. Only when he learns that his servant Pug is a legitimate devil does Fitzdottrel stop counterfeiting madness and expose the cozener. For a gull to expose a swindler is a major departure from Jonson's usual method. A Jonson gull usually remains a gull, past the play's end. This should have been especially true for Fitzdottrel, who declares: "I will be what I am." Fitzdottrel's sudden revelation of Meercraft's cozenage, with no word from Meercraft, points up Jonson's greater ethical concern in this play, and displays him as the stern moralist of his early period. This new sense of morality—or, perhaps, old sense of morality—is no accident of hasty writing, for it is reinforced when Jonson allows Fitzdottrel to escape cuckoldry. Wittipol, who had sought the virtue of Mistress Fitzdottrel, relinquishes his rights to the lady by claiming that he loves goodness more than beauty, a sentiment that somehow rings false when the goodness belongs to the wife of an unabashed fool who deserves his horns. By softening the punishment of the fool and exposing the rogue, Jonson displays a morality closer to Dekker's.

Pug is ineffectual in London, as Satan thought he would be. He is pathetically lacking in cleverness, and can invent no scheme that does not make him its victim. When he decides to act like a member of the London underworld by stealing the suit, purse, and money of Ambler, he is caught and thrown into a cell in Newgate. The body he occupies comes full circle round—it began at Tyburn and will end there. He fears what Satan will think. When Iniquity enters his cell, Pug blames Satan for his predicament.

> . . . He knew
> What I would suffer, when he tie'd me up thus
> In a rogues body: and he has (I thanke him)
> His tyrannous pleasure on me, to confine me
> To the unlucky carkasse of a *Cutpurse,*
> Wherein I could do nothing.

At this point Satan enters to chastise him:

> Impudent fiend,
> Stop thy lewd mouth. Doest thou not shame and tremble
> To lay thine owne dull damn'd defects upon
> An innocent case, there? Why thou heavy slave!
> The spirit, that did possesse that flesh before,
> Put more true life, in a finger, and a thumbe,
> Than thou in the whole Masse.
> (V,6,36-42)

He then ends an account of all the abuses that Pug suffered during his day in London with these words:

> Faith, would your predecessour,
> The *Cutpurse,* thinke you, ha' been so? Out upon thee,
> The hurt th'hast don, to let men know their strength,
> And that they are able to out-doe a *divel*
> Put in a body, will for ever be
> A scarre upon our Name! whom thou hast dealt with,
> Woman or man, this day, but have out-gone thee
> Some way, and most have prov'd the better fiendes?
> (V,6,55-65)

Pug, in complete disgrace, leaves the stage on the back of Iniquity.

The relationship between hell and the underworld, so frequent an association in the rogue pamphlets, is dramatized by Jonson. Satan chooses the body of a dead cutpurse as the receptacle of Pug's spirit. Pug himself becomes a thief, and his thievish activities lead him to Newgate. He is compared by Satan to the thief whose body he occupies, and he is abused in the comparison. Satan does not compare Pug to the play's live member of the underworld, Meercraft, but Jonson dramatizes their difference throughout the play. Meercraft is the play's real devil and outdoes Pug in every kind of villainy. The devil of hell is an ass, not the devil of the underworld. And, Fitzdottrel, the victim of the human devil's schemes, is also an ass. The projector, the gull, and the devil reflect one another's characters. Jonson demonstrates that the flesh is both more villainous than the spirit, and at least as foolish. But Jonson does more than this, for by allowing his audience to witness the activities of Pug in London, he proves that the real devil is of no consequence in a city of devils. Dekker had previously played with this idea in *If This Be Not a Good Play, the Devil Is In It*. Where fiends abound, a Pug can do little damage. Pug himself sums up this idea best when he states: "You talke of a University; why, *Hell* is/ A Grammar-schoole to this!"

In comparing Pug to the cutpurse whose body he occupied, Satan expresses a respect for the cleverness and skill of the London underworld which the audience shared. But the cutpurse was, significantly, hanged: a fate condoned by the audience. Jonson, in this play, is at one with the audience. His underworld, in the person of Meercraft, is an instrument of cozenage, ridiculing the folly of the Fitzdottrels of the world. But the fertile brain of Meercraft is not enough to allow him to escape exposure by his foolish victim. The Jonson of *The Alchemist* and *Bartholomew Fair* forced his audience to witness the antics of the underworld with a suspension of moral indictment. The Jonson of *The Devil is an Ass* witnesses the antics of Meercraft in the same climate of moral opinion as his audience. Nor is Meercraft as vital a character as the rogues of *The Alchemist* and *Bartholomew Fair*. Freda Townsend's opinion that after the "quicksilver cleverness of Face, Meercraft seems etiolate," [13] is correct. Jonson seems to have become disenchanted with the London underworld. Meercraft allows Jonson to point up the folly of his dupes, to be sure, but Jonson turns to the underworld of hell as his major instrument of satire against all of London. The London underworld has become as dead for Jonson as the body of his dead cutpurse, both revivified slightly with the help of the supernatural underworld, but dead nevertheless. Why Jonson abandoned the use of the underworld as his center of attraction—a structural device of proven success—why he allowed his fool to expose his projector, why he shifted back to the stern moralist after having become the genial observer is a mystery. Perhaps it is enough to say, to Jonson's credit, that he was forever experimenting with new methods to expose folly. But one must also say that when he abandoned the underworld as the attractive center of his comedy—attractive structurally and appealing enough to beguile the audience into investigating its own values—he abandoned his richest instrument of satire.

The Devil is an Ass, with its devil scenes looking back to an earlier dramatic tradition and with Jonson operating in a conventional climate of opinion, indicates the direction Jonson's career will take. In his last period Jonson deals with allegory and romance; in so doing he leaves behind him the Elizabethan underworld. Not one of the three plays he writes after his return to the stage in 1626 makes important use of the underworld. One, *The Staple of News,* does bring together cheater and victims, but the Staple office is not, as Herford and Simpson believe, "simply a variant of the Alchemist's Laboratory." [14] The Staple is not the structural center of the play, nor is Cymbal, who exploits the fools who visit the Staple, an underworld character. His preying upon the curiosity of his dupes is not a criminal offense. And his antics are not the play's central interest. The main plot does not deal with the knave-fool relationship; it concentrates upon the wooing of Penniboy Junior of Lady Pecunia, who is the play's center of attraction. Jonson here, as in *The Devil is an Ass,* does not allow his swindler to triumph; the Staple goes bankrupt.

It is in the Pecunia plot that an element of the Elizabethan underworld briefly enters the play. Penniboy's father disguises himself as a canter, a sturdy beggar taken out of the rogue pamphlets. He acts as a chorus throughout the play, uttering sententious sayings. In his rags he becomes Jonson's obvious mouthpiece in his attitude toward money:

> Why, that's the end of wealth! thrust riches outward,
> And remaine beggars within: contemplate nothing
> But the vile sordid things of time, place, money,
> And let the noble, and the precious goe,
> Vertue and honesty; hang 'hem; poore thinne membranes
> Of honour; who respects them? O, the *Fates!*
> How hath all just, true reputation fall'n,
> Since money, this base money 'gan to have any!
>
> (III,2,241-48)

He discovers his true identity when he can no longer endure his son's treatment of Lady Pecunia. Penniboy Canter takes charge of Pecunia, and leaves his son his vagabond's cloak.

The rags of a rogue serve a useful purpose; when Penniboy Jr. is seen wearing them in Act V he is a different person.

> Nay, they are fit, as they had been made for me,
> And I am now a thing, worth looking at!
> The same, I said I would be in the morning.
> No Rogue, at a *Comitia* of the *Canters,*
> Did ever there become his *Parents Robes*
> Better, than I do these: great foole! and begger!
>
> (V,1,1-6)

His appearance as a rogue makes him recognize his foolishness: "I now begin to see my vanity/ Shine in this Glasse, reflected by the foile!" In his great comedies the underworld was used to point up the folly of its victims; here Jonson uses the underworld's garments to allow a fool to recognize his own folly. The flesh and blood of the great comedies have been transformed to a cloak, in the same way that the play's characters have been transformed to semi-allegorical abstractions.

Both *The New Inn* and *The Magnetic Lady* are attempts to present a comedy of humours within a romantic context. In the former, Jonson presents a country setting, thereby giving himself no chance to provide his audience with the powerful depiction of London life which is one of the marks of his particular genius. In the latter, instead of an alchemist or a fair being the center of the play's activities, the audience finds, of all things, a lady—and not a very magnetic one at that. In neither play does the underworld enter.

IV

Focusing attention on Jonson's use of the Elizabethan underworld reveals much about the development of his art, for the underworld provided Jonson with his most effective instrument of satire and his most dynamic structural center. The emergence of his use of the underworld parallels his development and achievement. In his early plays, when he used the underworld merely for local color, and in his later plays, when he avoided the underworld, Jonson's comedy was at times successful, but never brilliant. In his middle period, the underworld supplied the stimulus for Jonson's greatest achievement. It became for him a realistic and vital center of operations, an instrument of cozenage, a moral reflector, and in *Bartholomew Fair* a rich symbol. It is true, as Harry Levin states, that beneath Jonson's writing "runs a broad substratum of journalism, of all the tracts, broadsides, and jest-books that had granted literary recognition to the London underworld before Jonson came along." [15] Most revealing, however, is what Jonson does with the attitude propagated by the products of this journalism. In making the underworld an instrument for his satire, and in allowing his underworld to go unpunished, Jonson inverts the conventional climate of opinion surrounding the underworld. In the Jonsonian world of cheaters and cheated, knaves and gulls, the gulls and the cheated become the objects of censure and ridicule. Of course, the activities of the underworld are exposed—placing them on the boards is in itself an exposure—but Jonson's true criticism falls on the greed, hypocrisy, and folly of the underworld's victims. For every alchemist there are many customers; at every fair there are many visitors. Jonson is interested in mocking the many, and in his mature period he discovered that the best way to do this was to bring the many to the few, to bring the cheated to the cheaters. The underworld, for Jonson, was a springe to catch woodcocks; naturally, he was more interested in the woodcocks than the springe.

Nor is the underworld of Jonson's plays a hateful world
preying upon honest citizens, as it often is in Dekker's plays.
It is at most a neutral world—and in *Bartholomew Fair* a
warmly human world—preying upon fools. At least one critic
could say that Jonson's rogues "perform rough justice upon
their dupes." [16] Jonson so effectively manipulates his underworld that the audience leaves the play thinking that the
victims are inferior to the cheaters. And the audience's
mocking laughter surrounds not Subtle or Edgworth
or Meercraft, but Mammon and Busy and Fitzdottrel. The
rogue pamphlets and Dekker are at one with the moral norm
of the audience and give the audience what it expects. Jonson's attitude toward the underworld, as his early plays and
The Devil is an Ass indicate, is also at one with the audience,
but in his middle period he does not give the audience what
it expects. He calculatingly, even arrogantly, jostles his audience's approved moral standards. In doing so his comedy
provides a valid satiric commentary on man's folly. At the
same time, he does not violate comic decorum. To have Edgworth caught picking Cokes' pocket and sent to the gallows,
to have Subtle and Face branded, to have Ursula and Doll
Common dragged along the streets in a cart, would be conforming to proper moral standards but would betray the
audience's sense of comic justice. It would be like locking
up Harpo Marx for his thefts or hanging the immoral Mac-
heath. The dramatist who sees humanity divided between
rogues and fools seems content to let his rogues play their
parts and go on their way, as do Subtle and Doll, or stay, as
do the Bartholomew birds.

5

William Shakespeare

Jonson's praise of Shakespeare—that he was "not of an age but for all time"—rings true. One does not turn to Shakespeare, as one often does to Jonson and Dekker, to learn about Elizabethan life. To be sure, he held the mirror of art up to that life, but what the mirror reflected was "nature." To investigate what the Shakespearean mirror reflects of one aspect of Elizabethan life—in this case, the underworld—is to discern more clearly the essentials of Shakespeare's art.

I

The origin of Shakespeare's use of the underworld as a separate distinct world occurs in a play that has no underworld at all, *A Midsummer Night's Dream*. Dekker had often divided society into the citizen world, court world, and underworld; Jonson usually looked at society as a clash between the world of rogues and the world of fools. Here, in *A Mid-summer Night's Dream,* Shakespeare for the first time separates society into parts, with each part essential to an organic whole. The plots of Theseus and Hippolita, the lovers, the fairies, and the mechanicals are so successfully interwoven that the audience admires the play's unity often without being aware of its geometric design. The wood in *A Midsummer Night's Dream,* as in many works of literature, is the world. It embraces both the ethereal Titania and the crude Bottom; indeed, they themselves embrace. The plots of the different worlds of the play not only dovetail; they reflect one another.[1] The role of Bottom and the mechanicals is especially note-worthy in this connection because the relationship between Bottom's world and the other worlds looks forward to the function of Falstaff's world in the *Henry IV* plays.

The rude mechanicals enter immediately after the first scene, which the idea of love pervades—Theseus and Hip-polita are preparing for their marriage; the young lovers are experiencing how rough the course of true love is. Bottom and company are also concerned with love, for they have decided to act out a tragic love affair for Theseus' wedding. Their foolish, but businesslike, activity in attempting to put on the play reflects the general activity concerned with the forthcoming marriage, the activity of the lovers, forever chas-ing one another and playing musical chairs, and the activity of the fairies, flitting across a moon-drenched wood. The story they choose to enact extends the love idea for it concerns Pyramus and Thisbe, whose love affair also demonstrates that true love does not run smooth. Their presentation not only makes the classic love story lamentably ludicrous, but pokes a mocking finger at the entire play's proceedings. Shakespeare causes Bottom and his crew to make the audience laugh at his own creation, the play itself. The debate by the mechanicals on how to bring the moon into the play is a revealing example of Shakespeare's use of Bottom's world to comment on the other worlds of the play. The moon shines throughout the play and all the lovers are aware of it. Theseus measures his oncoming marriage by the moon and regrets the slowness of its pace. Hippolita also talks about the moon, which will "behold the night/ Of our solemnities." Lysander and Hermia will meet secretly "when Phoebe doth behold/ Her silver visage in the watery glass." Oberon and Titania are "ill met by moonlight." And so on. Moonlight is constantly suggested, as one would expect in a play called *A Midsummer Night's Dream*.[2] However, although the moon shines on Athenian lovers, legendary heroes and supernatural fairies, it must be sought after by the mechanicals. "Find out moonshine, find out moonshine." They search for the moon in an almanac, of all things. Although the moon will be shining on the night of the performance, they will present the moon by having one of their group carry a lantern and a bush of thorns. The very moon which pervades the play's dreamlike atmosphere is literally and laughingly brought down to earth.

In *A Midsummer Night's Dream* Shakespeare plays upon all the strings of love; the Bottom plot allows Shakespeare to pluck the lowest string. In this play, Shakespeare's ability to fragment society and allow its parts to reflect one another meaningfully is seen for the first time.[3] His method in this comedy looks forward to the *Henry IV* plays, where society is once again divided, and where each element in that society serves as a significant reflector of every other element. Here the underworld plays an important part.

The events of *1 Henry IV* look back to the first part of the tetralogy, *Richard II*. There Shakespeare concentrated on Richard's character, the play being essentially the study

of a particular kind of king. The usurpation of the Crown by
Bolingbroke has great importance in the plot, but Shakespeare
does not dwell upon the idea of usurpation until he writes the
next two plays of the tetralogy, where the idea of usurpation
becomes forcefully connected with the idea of thievery.

Shakespeare directly looks forward to the *Henry IV* plays
in *Richard II* when Bolingbroke refers to his "unthrifty son":

> Inquire at London, 'mongst the taverns there,
> For there, they say, he daily doth frequent,
> With unrestrained loose companions,
> Even such, they say, as stand in narrow lanes,
> And beat our watch, and rob our passengers;
> Which he, young wanton and effeminate boy,
> Takes on the point of honour to support
> So dissolute a crew.[4]

Two scenes before this, however, a more indirect and more
interesting reference anticipates the goings-on in *Henry IV*.
Richard's Queen, when she sees her husband guarded, says to
him: "thou most beauteous inn,/ Why should hard-favour'd
grief be lodged in thee,/ When triumph is become an alehouse
guest?" (V,1,13-15). The Queen, comparing her husband
to Bolingbroke, thinks of a fair inn in constrast to an alehouse
where disorder reigns. Shakespeare in *Richard II* is interested
primarily in exploring how beauteous that inn is; in the
Henry IV plays his interest shifts to the alehouse, which becomes a symbol of disorder in England.

1 Henry IV contains four long accounts of Bolingbroke's
usurpation. The audience must never forget what Shakespeare
himself paid little attention to in *Richard II*—that Bolingbroke's seizure of the Crown of England was essentially an
act of thievery. This act results in a state of disorder in the
commonwealth, and Shakespeare uses the underworld to

reflect this disorder. As in *A Midsummer Night's Dream*, Shakespeare separates society into specific worlds, but the separation in *Henry IV* is based on politics, not love. The three worlds of the play are the court world, the rebel world, and the underworld, each meaningfully interacting with the others. The most obvious and most important aspect of the interaction between the royal world and the underworld is Prince Hal's connection with Falstaff and his cohorts.

The relationship between Hal and Falstaff has been the subject of many critical discussions. The crucial part of any of these discussions concerns Hal's rejection of Falstaff. The disturbances felt by Maurice Morgann and A. C. Bradley concerning the persecution of Falstaff are, in part, justified, because the audience does tend to sympathize with the fat knight. But, as J. Dover Wilson states, such an attitude is not the Elizabethan attitude. To him "the Falstaff-Hal plot embodies a composite myth which had been centuries amaking, and was for the Elizabethans full of meaning that has disappeared since then." [5] This myth involves Falstaff as the Devil of the miracle plays, the Vice of the moralities, the Riot of the interludes, in addition to the Fool, Buffoon, and Jester of folk-custom, with a strain of the *miles gloriosus* added. He believes, and in this he is in accord with Tillyard [6] and Traversi, [7] that Shakespeare prepares for the rejection and that it should come as no surprise to a reader who carefully looks at the scenes involving the future king and the "misleader of youth." The Elizabethans, to be sure, were able to discern parts, at least, of the "composite myth" that Wilson refers to, but perhaps their attitude towards him can be discovered more easily by thinking of Falstaff as, what he most obviously is, an underworld character. Considering him in terms of the underworld he represents will help to explain why the Elizabethans were able to enjoy the old rogue and at the

same time find his rejection not only convincing, but necessary.

The audience's first glimpse at the Falstaff-Hal relationship
comes in I,2. Falstaff begins the scene by asking what seems
to be a simple question calling for little else than a direct
answer: "Now, Hal, what time of day is it, lad?" But
no direct answer comes from Hal; instead he attacks the
character of Falstaff, indicating that for Falstaff Time is used
for wine, women, and song, that Time is not important for
him "unless hours were cups of sack and minutes capons and
clocks the tongues of bawds and dials the signs of leaping-
houses and the blessed sun himself a fair hot wench in flame-
coloured taffeta" (I,2,8-11). In this first speech, therefore,
the attitude of Hal to Falstaff is clear, for the Youth who
talks this way to his "misleader," the Youth who understands
the qualities of his misleader, is never in moral trouble. That
the recognition is true is confirmed by Falstaff himself—
"Indeed, you come near me now, Hal." He then identifies
himself as a member of the underworld: "for we that take
purses go by the moon and the seven stars, and not by Phoe-
bus." He goes on to romanticize his vocation:

Marry, then, sweet wag, when thou art king, let not us that are
squires of the night's body be called thieves of the day's beauty:
let us be Diana's foresters, gentlemen of the shade, minions of
the moon; and let men say we be men of good government,
being governed, as the sea is, by our noble and chaste mistress
the moon, under whose countenance we steal.

(I,2,25-33)

But the bubble of romance is burst immediately by Hal:

Thou sayest well, and it holds well too; for the fortune of us
that are the moon's men doth ebb and flow like the sea, being

governed, as the sea is, by the moon. As, for proof, now: a purse
of gold most resolutely snatched on Monday night and most
dissolutely spent on Tuesday morning; got with swearing "Lay
by" and spent with crying "Bring in"; now in as low an ebb
as the foot of the ladder and by and by in as high a flow as
the ridge of the gallows.

(I,2,34-43)

In the course of forty-three lines of the first exchange between Hal and Falstaff, Hal presents two speeches in which
he demonstrates that he clearly understands the nature of his
companion and the nature of the underworld. Although the
scene is bathed in apparent fellowship and laughter, the difference in attitude between the man who calls thieves "minions
of the moon" and the man who thinks of thieves and sees the
gallows is a great one—and it never changes throughout the
two *Henry IV* plays. Falstaff's question to Hal, "Shall there
be gallows standing in England when thou art king?" although
said with a smile perhaps, points to the failure of Falstaff to
see the wall that stands between him and Hal. For Hal, in this
very first exchange with Falstaff, emphasizes law and order
and the results of crime—thereby indicating from the beginning that he does not partake of the inherent values of Falstaff's tavern world. The audience should never fail to understand that Hal is merely "playing" Falstaff's friend, although
Falstaff himself fails to understand it. This is his greatest
failure, for the man who is not deceived about honor or war
or life is utterly deceived about himself in his relations with
the prince.

Talk about thieves and robbery takes up much of this
scene. A robbery is being planned. Poins, Falstaff remarks,
will tell them if "Gadshill have set a match." Poins himself is "the most omnipotent villain that ever cried 'Stand' to a
true man." The idea of true against false rings throughout

the scene and play, as is fitting in an England whose king
may not be a "true" king, whose prince may not be a
"true" prince—the emphasis in the term "heir apparent" is
often on "apparent." Falstaff hopes that "the true prince may,
for recreation sake, prove a false thief." And Hal does become a false thief, for he robs the thieves of their booty.
In the emphasis on thievery and in the true-false idea the underworld becomes a vehicle for demonstrating the disorder
in the realm and for illustrating that in many respects the
underworld and the court world overlap. That Hal is
spending his time with the underworld is the most obvious
manifestation of this overlapping. But Hal, although he is
with the underworld, is not of it. If the exchange between
Hal and Falstaff did not make this clear, the famous Hal
soliloquy does.

The first nine lines of the soliloquy pinpoint Hal's aliena-
tion from the world of Falstaff.

> I know you all, and will awhile uphold
> The unyoked humour of your idleness:
> Yet herein will I imitate the sun,
> Who doth permit the base contagious clouds
> To smother up his beauty from the world,
> That, when he please again to be himself,
> Being wanted, he may be more wonder'd at,
> By breaking through the foul and ugly mists
> Of vapours that did seem to strangle him.
>
> (I,2,218-226)

The soliloquy's beginning, "I know you all," had already
been fully demonstrated in his initial exchanges with Falstaff. That he will "imitate the sun" recalls an image so
pregnant in *Richard II* and so opposite to the moon image
associated with the underworld. That he will break through

"the foul and ugly mists" of the underworld vividly indicates his attitude toward the underworld. He ends the soliloquy with this pregnant couplet:

> I'll so offend, to make offense a skill;
> Redeeming time when men think least I will.
>   (I,2,239-40)

Time will be redeemed by Hal just when he can shine brightest. He will appear like the sun when he breaks away from the dark foul underworld, from the moon men. While England is in a state of disorder, while rebels have begun their intrigues, while Falstaff and his crew are planning a robbery, Hal stands apart, waiting to shine. During this wait Hal is clouded by the underworld around him. In the previous scene his father sees "dishonour" stain his brow; in the following scene Hotspur is consistently contemptuous of Hal— he would have him "poison'd with a pot of ale." Falstaff, when he plays Hal's father in II,4, presents the question puzzling all: "Shall the son of England prove a thief and take purses? . . . pitch doth defile; so doth the company thou keepest." The audience, however, knows that the pitch will be rubbed off at the proper time.

The first act presents the three worlds with which the next nine acts will deal, proceeding from the court world to the underworld to the rebel world, with Hal seen in the second scene and discussed in the first and third scenes, and with disorder the main element in each scene. These scenes are followed by the Carrier scene, usually dismissed as merely presenting some diversion for the rabble in the pit. But it is much more. The carriers, ready to start their work, complain that the ostler has not packed their horses. During the course of their complaining, filled with references to disease and urine, the second carrier says: "this house is turned upside down since Robin Ostler died." This is one of those Shakespearian lines that linger in the reader's mind; it is clearly the most forceful line in the scene, and it attaches to itself a distinct feeling for the past. Immediately before the carriers entered, the rebels were seen discussing Bolingbroke's usurpation and their future plans of rebellion. During the conversation between the carriers, Gadshill, a professional thief, enters, ready to set up the robbery mentioned in I,2. The juxtaposition of these scenes seems deliberate and tends to extend the usurpation idea—the King usurped the Crown, the rebels will attempt to steal it from the King, the professional thieves will rob a franklin. The court world, the rebels, and the underworld are one; England is in a state of disorder. Indeed, "the house is turned upside down."

Gadshill's conversation with the chamberlain strengthens the idea of the relationship between the underworld and the court world, for he boasts that he is "joined with . . . nobility and tranquillity, burgomasters and great oneyers, such as can hold in, such as will strike sooner than speak, and speak sooner than drink, and drink sooner than pray: and yet, 'zounds, I lie; for they pray continually to their saint, the commonwealth; or rather, not pray to her, but prey on her, for they ride up and down on her and make her their boots" (II,1,84-91). Here the alliance between the court world and the underworld is stated directly. Robbery seems to have royal patronage.

The robbery itself takes place in the next scene. When the robbers spot their prey, Bardolph exclaims: "there's money of the king's coming down the hill; 'tis going to the king's exchequer." To which Falstaff replies: "You lie, ye rogue; 'tis going to the king's tavern." The overlapping is obvious, for in time of disorder the tavern can be compared to the

exchequer. But in this very act of robbery Falstaff is deceived by Hal, because Hal and Poins rob the thieves. This
for the sake of the "good jest," to be sure, but also because
Hal is directly involved with the king's exchequer and only
an observer in the king's tavern. The jest provides laughter
in scene 4 of this act, and it is in this very scene that
Shakespeare makes sure that Hal tells the Sheriff looking for
the thieves that "the money shall be paid back again with
advantage." Hal must be completely clean.

The scene also gives the audience another reason for Hal's
association with the underworld, perhaps the most important
reason. Hal tells Poins: "I have sounded the very base
string of humility." This sounding by Hal is part of his
education. In Falstaff and his fellow thieves Hal is able
to observe at first hand the products and propagators of
disorder. He is learning to understand all men as they are,
including the lowest members of society. In his relationship
with the underworld he deliberately sounds the base string.
His statement, later in the scene, that he is "now of all humours
that have showed themselves humours since the old days of
goodman Adam" suggests that he is completing his education,
for to be of all humours is, essentially, to understand all
humours, an admirable quality in a king.

That Falstaff thrives on disorder is emphasized throughout
the play. His attitude toward the rebels is significant in this
connection—"Well, God be thanked for these rebels, they
offend none but the virtuous: I laud them, I praise them"
(III,3,213-15). When Hal relates that he is good friends
with his father "and may do anything," Falstaff says: "Rob
me the exchequer the first thing thou doest, and do it with
unwashed hands too." In IV, 2 Falstaff points out that he has
"misused the king's press damnably," for he has exchanged
soldiers for money. This practice, attacked by the Statutes of

the Realm, would have helped to alienate the audience from Falstaff. The soldiers that he did get came from prison; they are not the best kind of fighting men for England. Fighting in the wars will not, of course, stop them from stealing, for "they'll find linen enough in every hedge" to supply them with the clothes they lack. But it is at the Battle of Shrewsbury that Falstaff becomes a complete symbol of irresponsibility, and it is there that Hal becomes most disgusted with him. When Hal draws a bottle of sack from Falstaff's case instead of a pistol, he exclaims: "What, is it a time to jest and dally now?" Hal knows when the time is right for play and when for war, but Falstaff does not. Hal throws the bottle at him and leaves; this act itself is a rejection.

Falstaff and his cohorts are the obvious thieves in the play—" 'tis my vocation." But the thief idea is played upon by Shakespeare throughout, so that it becomes a leading motif—in big issues, as when the rebels, with their map before them, divide England into three parts, like thieves dividing their booty; and in small matters, as when Lady Percy playfully tells Hotspur, "Lie still, ye thief." Henry IV, giving his son an account of the usurpation, uses this interesting phrase: "And then I stole all courtesy from heaven." The word "stole" indicates that morality for Henry IV is a matter of expediency, as it is for Falstaff. The royal world and the underworld, represented by Henry IV and Falstaff, vie for the attention and affection of Hal, and each is an exponent of the kind of expediency that Hal will display as king. The underworld father of Hal and the royal-world father are, indeed, similar. When the underworld father poses as the court father in the "play extempore" he plays on the theme of Hal's keeping bad company and attempts to defend himself. Both Falstaff and Henry IV realize that Hal's relationship with the underworld is detrimental to his reputation.

There is also a correspondence between Falstaff and the leading member of the rebel world, Hotspur. True, they represent extremes of behavior. Falstaff is commonsensical; honor for him is a mere word. Hotspur is impractical and romantic; to pluck bright honor he would go to the moon. One is heroic; the other is unheroic. Yet, despite their many differences as individuals, the worlds which they represent are similar in their reliance on disorder and in their disregard for the realm. One thief will take on all opponents openly and directly in civil war, even before reinforcements come. The other thief will hide behind a bush at night to wait for unsuspecting prey. But both cause chaos in the commonwealth, and both, despite some glowing personal attributes, must be judged as thieves.

In one respect or another, most of the leading characters in the play are thieves, from the highest to the lowest. It is to the thief Falstaff that Shakespeare pays most attention, and Shakespeare invests him with so much humanity that merely calling him a thief, or a Vice, or Riot, minimizes the worth of this full character. Falstaff possesses a sharp intelligence, a brilliant wit, an ability to see through the hypocrisies of life. As Traversi states, he "proves, besides a living picture of disorder, a valid comic commentary." [8] He is the supreme parodist. He is able to mock, he is able to laugh, he is able to enjoy the experience called life. His statement, "Banish plump Jack, and banish all the world," rings true. And yet he must be banished. For plump Jack, invested with so much wit and good fellowship, remains an underworld character.[9] His wit may be able to minimize his cowardice and lying, but it cannot change what he is. As a member of the underworld and, in part, as a vestige from the morality tradition, he presented a double image to the Elizabethans. As Chapter 1 has demonstrated, the Elizabethans were able to enjoy the antics of the members of the underworld, but they knew that the gallows waited at the end of every devious, though jolly, path. In addition, the underworld in the morality tradition served both as a symbol of evil and a source of comedy. The quality of dual awareness surrounds the large figure of Falstaff. He evokes two responses from the audience at the same time. The rich ambiguity surrounding the underworld, discussed in Chapters 1 and 2, finds its physical embodiment in Falstaff. To the Elizabethans the rejection of that very Falstaff who provides so much humor would have been natural and necessary. To make it even more necessary Shakespeare presents a more debased Falstaff in Part 2 of *Henry IV,* and a more diseased underworld.

As in I,2 of Part 1, so too in I,2 of Part 2, a question by Falstaff begins the scene. He asks his page—for Hal is not often with him in Part 2—"Sirrah, you giant, what says the doctor to my water?" The page answers. "He said, sir, the water itself was a good healthy water; but, for the party that owed it, he might have more diseases than he knew for." The disease note is sounded immediately, and it persists throughout—in the underworld and in the commonwealth. The king tells Warwick that "the body of the kingdom" is "foul": "what rank diseases grow,/ And with what danger, near the heart of it" (III,1,39-40). This, because of the activities of the rebels. The rank diseases also grow in the tavern world, typified by Falstaff's relationship to Doll Tearsheet.

Whereas in Part 1 the audience hears about Falstaff's wenching, in Part 2 the audience sees him bounce a whore on his fleshy knee. His first words to Doll concern disease— "we catch of you, Doll, we catch of you" (II,4,49). But this does not stop him from associating with her, for the

Falstaff of Part 2 is lecherous, and he seems much older than the Falstaff of Part 1. Poins makes the following judgment of Falstaff: "Is it not strange that desire should so many years outlive performance?" Doll herself feels the same way about Falstaff, for in a gush of her special kind of sentimentality she says to him: "Thou whoreson little tidy Bartholomew boar-pig, when wilt thou leave fighting o' days and foining o' nights, and begin to patch up thine old body for heaven?" (II,4,250-53). Falstaff says "I am old, I am old," but this recognition seems to spur him on in his relations with Doll—"it grows late; we'll to bed." The prince then enters to tell him that he must go to the wars. The fact that rebels are causing chaos in the commonwealth does not disturb him so much as his having to leave before he tastes "the sweetest morsel," Doll Tearsheet. He leaves, but immediately Doll is sent for. The audience can be sure that lechery preceded duty.

Falstaff is not the only old man, nor is he the only lecher, in a play where physical degeneration signifies moral degeneration. The rebels of Part 2 are older than those of Part 1. Henry IV is sick, and soon to die. And old Shallow can only think of the good old days. When he does reminisce with Falstaff he thinks about the whore, Jane Nightwork. When Falstaff tells him, "We have heard the chimes at midnight, Master Shallow," he is talking about the past for Shallow, but his own present. For Falstaff continues to hear the chimes at midnight.

Another old man enters the play, and he serves as Falstaff's opposite. Their professions alone would make them enemies—one is Lord Chief Justice and the other is a thief; one is a symbol of order and rule, the other a symbol of disorder and riot. The royal world, which was a parallel world to the underworld in Part 1, is now becoming a con-

trasting world. When Hal becomes king he will supposedly
have to choose between the two men—but in reality there
is no choice at all. The audience knows, as Hal knows,
upon whom Hal will lean. Hal is never engaged in a moral
struggle; he is not Everyman pulled by the good and bad
angels. He has rejected his ill angel long before the final rejection. The Lord Chief Justice does not know this. When
he learns that Hal has become king, he states: "O God, I
fear all will be overturn'd!" (V,2,19). A king who has
companions in the underworld will cause the house to be
turned upside down. This is exactly what Falstaff is depending upon, for thieves can thrive when the time is unquiet.
Falstaff will become, as Pistol states and Falstaff believes,
"one of the greatest men in the realm," now that Hal is king.
Falstaff's reaction to the news is indicative of his basic mis-
conception about Hal and his love of disorder and anarchy.
Before rushing to court he says: "Let us take any man's
horses; the laws of England are at my commandment. Blessed
are they that have been my friends; and woe to my lord
chief-justice!" (V,3,143-45). When he reaches the court he
tells Pistol he will "deliver" Doll Tearsheet, who in the preceding scene was seen dragged across the stage by beadles
because "there hath been a man or two lately killed about
her." The hand of law and order is already functioning;
one of Falstaff's crew has been seized. Falstaff believes that
he can twist that hand to his own will. Then comes the rejection.

Both parts of *Henry IV* have been leading to this rejection.
It comes as no surprise; the scales have been tipped against
Falstaff from the beginning. Yet, the terms of the rejection are
somewhat puzzling. Hal claims that Falstaff was "the tutor
and feeder" of his riots and one of his "misleaders." (In his
first exchange with Falstaff, the Lord Chief Justice said he

"misled the youthful prince.") However, Hal was never misled. To be sure, this is the proper time to denounce publicly his companions of the underworld, to break through the "foul and ugly mists," but some of the terms of the denunciation are false. The sun has spots—but it remains the sun. Falstaff and the underworld must be banished if England is to enjoy the peace that only order can bring. The underworld must also be understood for what it is, and Henry V has this understanding, for he studied it at first hand. Warwick had predicted that Hal "but studies his companions" and that he will "cast off his followers." This Hal does, in terms that are unequivocal. He has attained, by experience, some of the wisdom necessary for kingship.

In *2 Henry IV* Falstaff has become old, lecherous, filled with disease, a symbol of disorder, and lacking in some of the comic energy he had in Part 1. Shakespeare makes his rejection easy, and complete. For the Falstaff who could talk his way out of every difficult situation is not allowed to speak. His broken sentence—"My lord, my lord——"—is never completed. And when his tongue stops, so does his heart, as the Hostess reports in *Henry V*.

The underworld of the *Henry IV* plays is present in *Henry V*, but with a difference. Whereas in *Henry IV* the underworld is a structural element which serves first as a parallel to and then as a contrast to the royal world, in *Henry V* it is absorbed by the royal world—for two reasons. First, the new King Henry, in his ideality and forcefulness, sweeps everything and everyone along with him. Second, and more important, the underworld of the *Henry IV* plays has lost its leader. Falstaff is gone, and so the members of the tavern group seem like a circumference without a center. Their first appearance in II,1 shows them quarreling. Pistol and Nym, a new member of the group, are enraged at one another because the Hostess, who was "troth-plight" to Nym, had married Pistol. In the course of their exchange, mention is made of Falstaff's former whore-friend, Doll Tearsheet. Pistol to Nym:

> O hound of Crete, think'st thou my spouse to get?
> No; to the spital go,
> And from the powdering-tub of infamy
> Fetch forth the lazar kite of Cressid's kind,
> Doll Tearsheet she by name, and her espouse.
> (II,1,77-81)

The powdering-tub and lazar suggest disease, but the tub and the spital suggest a chance for cure. Diseases are cured in this play, for England is healthier with Henry V ruling. Bardolph comes between Pistol and Nym, uttering these words: "Come, shall I make you two friends? We must to France together: why the devil should we keep knives to cut one another's throats?" This is an interesting sentiment; there is no reason for Englishmen, even thieves, to fight one another when Frenchmen are available. The wars will also provide them with an opportunity to carry on their vocations. As Pistol states, "Let us to France; like horse-leeches, my boys,/ To suck, to suck, the very blood to suck!" (II,3,57-8).

In France the Boy, who presents some of Falstaff's sentiments throughout the play ("Would I were in an alehouse in London! I would give all my fame for a pot of ale and safety."), reports on the activities of the underworld:

They will steal anything, and call it purchase. Bardolph stole a lute-case, bore it twelve leagues, and sold it for three half-pence. Nym and Bardolph are sworn brothers in filching, and in Calais they stole a fire-shovel: I knew by that piece of service the men would carry coals. They would have me as familiar with

men's pockets as their gloves or their handkerchers: which makes
much against my manhood, if I should take from another's
pocket to put into mine; for it is plain pocketing up of wrongs.
I must leave them, and seek some better service: their villainy goes against my weak stomach, and therefore I must cast
it up.

(III,2,44-57)

They will pay for their villainy. Three scenes later, Pistol
reports that Bardolph must be hanged because he stole a
pax. The incident is reported to Henry V by Fluellen. "I
think the duke has lost never a man, but one that is like to be
executed for robbing a church, one Bardolph." The righteous
Henry states: "We would have all such offenders so cut
off." He later states that war is God's "beadle, war is his
vengeance; so that here men are punished for before-breach
of the king's laws in now the king's quarrel" (IV,1,180-2).
This proves true for the members of the underworld, for
Bardolph and Nym are both hanged, and Pistol would be
also, according to the Boy, "if he durst steal anything ad-
venturously." Pistol, after being forced by Fluellen to eat
leek, leaves the stage after he utters these words:

> Doth Fortune play the huswife with me now?
> News have I, that my Nell is dead i' the spital
> Of malady of France;
> And there my rendezvous is quite cut off.
> Old I do wax; and from my weary limbs
> Honour is cudgelled. Well, bawd I'll turn,
> And something lean to cutpurse of quick hand.
> To England will I steal, and there I'll steal:
> And patches will I get unto these cudgell'd scars,
> And swear I got them in the Gallia wars.
>
> (V,1,85-94)

Pistol, the only survivor of the Falstaff crew, will return to England to steal.

It is significant that the underworld which ran rampant in *Henry IV* is eliminated, except for one member, in *Henry V*. The ideal king has made good "use" of his "wilder days," as he puts it. Law and order will, for the most part, prevail in England under King Harry. But Shakespeare, the realist, knows that the underworld will never be completely eliminated, so he allows Pistol to remain alive. Although God punishes his offenders, as Harry states, there is still one vestige of Falstaff's world roaming—the most cowardly of all, but alive to steal. Ambidexter's "cosin cutpurse" will ever be at hand.

In both parts of Henry IV the underworld is a dramatic world in constant interaction with the court world. It both reflects and is emblematic of the disorder in the commonwealth, and serves as an important part of the education of a prince. And it has as its leader one of Shakespeare's great characters, Falstaff. The vigor of this world dissipates when Falstaff leaves it, when it must operate in an England that is not turned upside down, when usurpation is trying to be forgotten. This happens in *Henry V*.

In the *Henry IV* plays, as in *A Midsummer Night's Dream*, Shakespeare divides society in order to comment on it. The underworld is important as a structural element in the plays; it serves as a reflector of the court and rebel worlds. When the rebels are destroyed and the court world is cleansed, the underworld no longer can serve as a reflector; it loses its structural function. But whether or not the underworld is a structual entity, Shakespeare's attitude toward it is essentially serious and moral in his history plays, where the peace and safety of England is the ultimate issue. The underworld is an ever-present threat to the realm. It can be a source of laughter—as it is in rogue pamphlet, morality play, and Falstaff—but it must be recognized as a fundamental evil.

II

The idea of the underworld as a world of evil is traditional. As Chapters 3 and 4 have demonstrated, Dekker and Jonson make much use of the traditional idea. So too does Shakespeare, but there is a vast difference in his artistic treatment of the idea. His first important use of the underworld as image and idea occurs in *Hamlet*.

The idea of the underworld appears in *Hamlet* in crucial places, especially the idea of whore which serves as a motif throughout the play. Small wonder, for one of the two leading themes in the play concerns the infidelity of Hamlet's mother. Even before Hamlet learns about his father's murder he is a disturbed young man because he is disillusioned with his mother's remarriage. When the Ghost reveals to Hamlet the terrible past, he is at least as disturbed about his mother's adultery as he is about his uncle's villainy. "O most pernicious woman!" comes before "O villain, villain, smiling, damned villain!" To Hamlet his mother is forever stained; and that he can never remove the stain—regardless of his revengeful actions toward Claudius—is the basic source of his moral frustration. The whore idea, therefore, naturally comes into play when Hamlet speaks, but it is not confined to Hamlet alone.

In II,2 Polonius, testing the madness of Hamlet, asks him the question most madmen are first asked: "Do you know me, my lord?" Hamlet answers, "Excellent well, you are a fishmonger." The answer makes audiences laugh, because a fishmonger is a low vocation and, more important, a fishmonger is a cant word for pander or pimp, a fishmonger's daughter being a synonym for prostitute. This is playful, but the allusion is interesting—first, because Polonius sounded very much like a pander when he said, a few lines earlier, that he would "loose" his daughter to Hamlet, and second, because Ophelia, in Hamlet's mind, will take on the characteristics of Hamlet's tainted mother. Being a woman, Ophelia will be condemned with all of whorish womankind. This becomes obvious in the nunnery scene, where nunnery, in addition to its normal use, also means brothel. After Ophelia's guilty answer "At home, my lord" to Hamlet's question "Where's your father?" Hamlet becomes enraged. His "Get thee to a nunnery" takes on all the force of his sending her to a brothel, especially when it is followed by:

> I have heard of your paintings too, well enough; God has given you one face, and you make yourselves another: you jig, you amble, and you lisp, and nickname God's creatures, and make your wantonness your ignorance. Go to, I'll no more on 't; it hath made me mad. I say, we will have no more marriages: those that are married already, all but one, shall live; the rest shall keep as they are. To a nunnery, go.
> (III,1,148-57)

Here the familiar "thee" becomes the general "you," and all of womankind takes on the characteristics of the whore, especially the falsity that the "painting" idea so vividly accentuates.

In the bedroom scene (III,4) the whore idea comes to a meaningful climax. Here Hamlet, face to face with his mother, alone with her for the first time, unburdens himself of all his feelings against her. He reminds her of her act that "takes off the rose/ From the fair forehead of an innocent love/ And sets a blister there," an act which brands her as a harlot. He says that her "reason pandars will," for the

situation in which a sexual kind of perversion is taking place
calls to Hamlet's mind the figure of a pander. In continuing
his chastisement he utters the following words:

> Nay, but to live
> In the rank sweat of an enseamed bed,
> Stew'd in corruption, honeying and making love
> Over the nasty sty, . . .
>
> (III,4,92-95)

Here the stews and disease and sexual disgust find their most
forceful expression, and it is here that Gertrude finally realizes
that Hamlet knows of her adultery. Gertrude asks him to
"speak no more," but Hamlet must purge himself of all his
thoughts about his mother's whorish behavior. He goes on
and on and on.

But this purgation does not allow Hamlet to forget his
mother's whorishness; it gives him only temporary relief.
When he refers to Claudius in V,2, he says: "He that hath
kill'd my king and whored my mother." And in the previous
scene, when Hamlet is contemplating Yorick's skull, he says:
"Now get you to my lady's chamber, and tell her, let her
paint an inch thick, to this favour she must come" (V,1,213).
Here woman and painting and death are combined, and the
woman is probably a whore. Hamlet's situation comes to
mind when Laertes, in the heat of his excitement for revenge,
utters these words:

> That drop of blood that's calm proclaims me bastard,   ,
> Cries cuckold to my father, brands the harlot
> Even here, between the chaste unsmirched brow
> Of my true mother.
>
> (IV,5,117-20)

Hamlet's father *was* a cuckold, and harlot *is* branded on his mother's brow.

Shakespeare makes much use of the whore idea in connection with Gertrude, but the idea is too potent to be confined to her alone. Hamlet, in soliloquy, scolding himself for his lack of gall, compares himself to the lowest of human kind, the underworld. "O, what a rogue and peasant slave am I." But this is not enough chastisement, for he also compares himself to a "whore," a "drab"—what is for him the worst of epithets because of his mother.

The play's most important whore image comes from the mouth of Claudius. After Polonius tells Ophelia to read the book of devotion and remarks that "with devotion's visage/ And pious action we do sugar o'er/ The devil himself," Claudius utters the following aside:

> O, 'tis too true!
> How smart a lash that speech doth give my conscience!
> The harlot's cheek, beautied with plastering art,
> Is not more ugly to the thing that helps it
> Than is my deed to my most painted word:
> O heavy burden!
>
> (III,1,49-54)

This is the first time in the play that Claudius reveals his guilt. The harlot-paint image is suited perfectly to indicate hypocrisy in a play filled with contrasts between appearance and reality. That the image comes from Claudius himself reveals that he is an atypical villain, not delighting in his villainy.

The whore idea, therefore, so pregnant in connection with Gertrude, is used by both of the mighty opposites—each chastises himself for acting like a whore.

Other underworld images, not associated with the whore,

are also woven into the play. Hamlet refers to Claudius as "A cutpurse of the empire and the rule,/ That from a shelf the precious diadem stole,/ And put it in his pocket!" (III, 4,99-101). The image is interesting because it informs the audience of Hamlet's attitude toward Claudius' "election" to the crown. That he associates Claudius with a thief calls to mind the thief idea connected with another stealer of the crown, Henry IV.

When he is dying, Hamlet utters that "this fell sergeant, death,/ Is strict in his arrest." Here death is presented as a sheriff's officer making an arrest, a final arrest, of Hamlet the rogue. The "sweet prince," it seems, is a rogue and peasant slave to the end.

In the world of Denmark, a loving wife and mother gathers to herself the qualities of a whore. A pure young girl is told to go to a nunnery, and eventually goes to a muddy death singing bawdy songs. A crown is snatched by a pickpurse, who considers himself as false as a painted whore. A noble prince compares himself to a whore and rogue. In a state that is rotten the high and the mighty, the pure and the stained, become members of the underworld, and no one escapes the final arrest by death.

In *Hamlet* the underworld is part of the fabric of Shakespeare's art. He has taken the Dekkerian image and used it as a kind of background for the play's action. In *Othello* Shakespeare not only uses the idea as a background but, in one scene, acts out the image and dramatizes the idea. The whore idea is significant in a play which deals with a woman's purity. Reference to the word whore or a synonym occurs twenty-two times; distinct whore imagery occurs twelve times. The combined total of whore references and associations is greater in *Othello* than in any other Shakespeare play. And the play contains a whore as a character. It is in III,3 that

the whore idea begins to take on its full force, because in that
scene Iago's poison begins to work on Othello's mind.
Before then, however, another underworld element, the thief
idea, comes into play in connection with Othello's "theft"
of Desdemona.

The shouts of Iago beneath Brabantio's window pierce
the play's dark whispering beginning.

> Awake! what, ho, Brabantio! thieves! thieves! thieves!
> Look to your house, your daughter and your bags!
> Thieves! thieves!

(I,1,79-81)

Iago, hidden in the dark, tells Brabantio that he has been
"robb'd" of his daughter. Iago's malignity is effective from
the very beginning of the play, because Brabantio, when he
confronts Othello, picks up the thief idea: "Down with him,
thief!" and "O thou foul thief, where hast thou stow'd my
daughter?" In the council chamber Brabantio once again
insists that Desdemona is "stol'n from me." After Desdemona
recites that Othello is her husband by choice, Brabantio is
despondent. The Duke, to assuage Brabantio's grief, says:
"The robb'd that smiles steals something from the thief;/ He
robs himself that spends a bootless grief" (I,3,208-9). The
thief idea, planted by Iago, grows in Brabantio's mind, becomes part of the atmosphere of Act I, and is used by the
play's highest official. Another underworld idea will be
planted by Iago, this time in the mind of the play's tragic
hero, and it will poison the entire play's atmosphere.

On line 35 of III,3 Iago begins his assault on Othello's
mind with the subtly half-muffled "Ha! I like not that" as
Cassio leaves the company of Desdemona. On line 476, four
lines before the scene's end, Othello refers to Desdemona as
a "lewd mix!"—"O damn her!" Between these two lines

the audience witnesses Iago's manipulation of Othello, a supreme achievement by the apostle of evil. The play's disease imagery, which infects the atmosphere of the whole play, forcefully begins when Othello's suspicions begin to take shape. "I had rather be a toad,/ And live upon the vapour of a dungeon,/ Than keep a corner in the thing I love/ For others' uses. Yet, 'tis the plague of great ones." And when he turns to Iago in anger, Othello uses the word which will ring throughout the remaining acts: "Villain, be sure thou prove my love a whore." He who had said "to be once in doubt/ Is once to be resolved" utters the word "whore" in reference to the purest of women.

At the end of the following scene the play's real whore, Bianca, enters. She and Cassio exchange some words, and then Cassio gives her the handkerchief that he found in his room in order for her to copy the embroidery.

BIANCA: O Cassio, whence came this?
          This is some token from a newer friend:
          To the felt absence now I feel a cause:
          Is't come to this? Well, well.
CASSIO: Go to, woman!
          Throw your vile guesses in the devil's teeth,
          From whence you have them. You are jealous now
          That this is from some mistress, some remembrance,
          No, in good troth, Bianca.
                    (III,4,180-7)

The word "jealous" is important here, for the green-eyed monster lurks in the low as well as the high. This becomes accentuated in IV,1, when Bianca enters again while Iago and Cassio are feeding the onlooker Othello's mind with more "proof" of Desdemona's whorishness. Bianca is fuming with **rage and jealousy.**

Let the devil and his dam haunt you! What did you mean by that same handkerchief you gave me even now? I was a fine fool to take it. I must take out the work? —A likely piece of work, that you should find it in your chamber, and not know who left it there! This is some minx's token, and I must take out the work? There; give it your hobby-horse: wheresoever you had it, I'll take out no work in 't.

(IV,1,153-61)

After a few more words she leaves. Her entrance here serves the action in that it prepares for the culmination of Iago's proof. But Shakespeare had another reason for her appearance at this time. Her jealousy surrounded by the scenes showing the jealousy of Othello serves to suggest that the noble Othello, in his jealousy, is acting like a common strumpet. Bianca's very words, "This is some minx's token," recall Othello's earlier "Damn her, lewd minx!" (The word "minx" occurs twice in this play; only three times in all of Shakespeare's plays.) Whereas Hamlet laments that he unpacks his heart with words, like a whore, Othello, in his passion, *does* unpack his heart with the words of the onstage whore, Bianca.

But Shakespeare gives Bianca's role a complexity that one begins to expect in his treatment of the underworld. For Bianca, the very whore who reflects Othello's degradation, is, as her name suggests, white. She is truly in love with Cassio, is genuinely distressed when she finds him wounded, and is maligned by Iago. She is, in respect to her love for Cassio, an honest whore, and reflects the honesty of the wife-called-whore Desdemona. Her dramatic function, therefore, is important. She not only serves the plot, but is used by Shakespeare as a reflector of *both* Othello and Desdemona. As a jealous strumpet, she is black; as a devoted lover, she is white. Shakespeare has attached to his underworld character a significant ambivalence.

The idea of Othello's degeneration is reinforced in IV,2, where Othello becomes a customer in a brothel of his own devising, with Emilia acting as bawd and Desdemona as whore. In this scene Shakespeare makes a new and unusual use of the underworld, dramatizing an image that is in a character's mind. The connection between Desdemona and whore is so strong for Othello, his perversion is so great, that his visit to Desdemona becomes a visit to a brothel. When Desdemona enters, she asks Othello: "My lord, what is your will?" Her first words fit the brothel idea perfectly. Othello's answer, "Pray, chuck, come hither" plays on the word chuck, which means both dear one and whore. Desdemona then utters another suggestive line: "What is your pleasure?" When Othello turns to the bawd Emilia, he says:

> Some of your function, mistress;
> Leave procreants alone and shut the door;
> Cough or cry 'hem', if any body come:
> Your mystery, your mystery: nay, dispatch.
>
> (IV,2,27-30)

Emilia leaves, and Othello turns to Desdemona to tell her of her falsity. He finally blurts out:

> Was this fair paper, this most goodly book,
> Made to write 'whore' upon? What committed!
> Committed! O thou public commoner!
> I should make very forges of my cheeks,
> That would to cinders burn up modesty,
> Did I but speak thy deeds. What committed!
> Heaven stops the nose at it, and the moon winks,
> The bawdy wind that kisses all it meets
> Is hush'd within the hollow mine of earth,
> And will not hear it. What committed!
> Impudent strumpet!
>
> (IV,2,71-81)

Her "By heaven, you do me wrong." does not stop his relentless attack. It merely changes his tone: "Are not you a strumpet?" "What, not a whore?" "Is't possible?" "I cry you mercy, then:/ I took you for that cunning whore of Venice/ That married with Othello." He then calls in the bawd Emilia, gives her money in payment for services, and leaves. In his playlet Othello has become a frequenter of brothels, and has reduced the symbol of pure love to a representative of the underworld and animal behavior. He is now compared by Emilia to a "beggar in his drink." Othello has reached his lowest moral depth—he has the passion of a strumpet, he is a brothel visitor, and he behaves like a beggar. He has symbolically acted out his spiritual death.

That Desdemona is a whore is ingrained in Othello's diseased mind. When he notices the wounded Cassio, he praises honest Iago, and then says: "strumpet, I come." He is on his way to kill Desdemona. In the death scene he calls her "strumpet" twice before he stifles her. And after her death he tells Emilia "she was a whore." Once the idea that Desdemona is a whore takes possession of him, Othello's world is shattered. Chaos comes again, and Desdemona's death is inevitable. In a later play a pure Marina will be able to demonstrate her purity in an onstage brothel, but in *Othello* the pure Desdemona can demonstrate nothing in the brothel of Othello's mind. She goes to her smothered death in innocence and ignorance.

Having used the underworld as image and idea in *Hamlet* and *Othello,* and having dramatized the image in one scene of *Othello,* Shakespeare goes on to make the image a form of symbolic disguise in *King Lear*. In a play that explores the relations between man and his moral universe Shakespeare presents the highest and the lowest, and causes them to meet on common ground. For the highest he chose King Lear, a

figure steeped in ancient mythology; for the lowest he chose
Tom o' Bedlam, the basest of underworld characters—naked
as the air that surrounds him, dirty as the road he tramps,
and mad as the chaotic universe in which he groans his particular plight.

The play's first Tom o' Bedlam reference comes from the
mouth of Edmund. After Edmund's famous denial of the
power of the stars, Edgar enters and Edmund begins his
villainous machinations—"my cue is villainous melancholy,
with a sigh like Tom o' Bedlam" (I,2,148). He will sigh in
order to trick his brother. A fleeting reference, to be sure,
but interesting because it will be Edmund's brother who will
sigh like Tom o' Bedlam throughout the play.

In II,3 Edgar reveals his plan to disguise as Tom:

> Whiles I may 'scape
> I will preserve myself: and am bethought
> To take the basest and most poorest shape
> That ever penury, in contempt of man,
> Brought near to beast: my face I'll grime with filth:
> Blanket my loins; elf all my hair in knots;
> And with presented nakedness out-face
> The winds and persecutions of the sky.
> The country gives me proof and precedent
> Of Bedlam beggars, who, with roaring voices,
> Strike in their numb'd and mortified bare arms
> Pins, wooden pricks, nails, sprigs of rosemary;
> And with this horrible object, from low farms,
> Poor pelting villages, sheep-cotes, and mills,
> Sometime with lunatic bans, sometime with prayers,
> Enforce their charity. Poor Turlygod! poor Tom!
> That's something yet: Edgar I nothing am.
>
> (II,3,5-21)

The country gives him precedent because Abraham men

were wandering through England for a long time. They were described by the rogue pamphleteers in much the same terms that Edgar uses. True Abraham men were legitimate beggars, but those who disguised themselves as Abraham men for profit were rogues. They were the most wretched members of the underworld.

Before Edgar appears as Tom o' Bedlam in III,4 the beggar idea achieves significance in connection with Lear. When Regan asks her father why he needs retainers, Lear answers:

> O, reason not the need: our basest beggars
> Are in the poorest thing superfluous:
> Allow not nature more than nature needs,
> Man's life 's cheap as beasts.
>   (II,4,267-270)

Here Lear alludes to beggars and beasts in referring to what man needs biologically and what man needs spiritually. He will learn to understand the difference between the biological and spiritual when he confronts the beggar-beast directly.

When Lear confronts Tom, Lear's education begins, for he will learn about the nature of man from the lowest of men. When he sees Tom, half-naked and filthy, Lear immediately thinks of his own situation. "What, have his daughters brought him to this pass?/ Couldst thou save nothing? Didst thou give all?" (III,4,65-66). After talk about daughters and brothels, Lear seems to take another look at Tom, and utters these important words:

Why, thou wert better in thy grave than to answer with thy uncovered body this extremity of the skies. Is man no more than this? Consider him well. Thou owest the worm no silk, the beast no hide, the sheep no wool, the cat no perfume. Ha! here's three on 's are sophisticated! Thou art the thing itself: un-

accomodated man is no more but such a poor, bare, forked
animal as thou art. Off, off, you lendings! come, unbutton
here.

(III,4,105-15)

Lear then rips off his clothes. When chaos is come—the
storm rages without and within—the unaccomodated man
must reign and must be recognized as the bare forked animal
he is. Lear is beginning to recognize essentials, "the thing
itself." His tearing off the clothes is an act of madness, but
at the same time it is a gesture of realization. Lear has profited
from his contact with Tom o' Bedlam.

In fact, Tom o' Bedlam, serving as a symbol of unaccomodated man, becomes for Lear a teacher and philosopher.
When Gloucester wishes to bring Lear to shelter, the mad
king says: "First let me talk with this philosopher" (III,4,
159). A few lines later he calls Tom "Noble philosopher."
In this connection, the words of Regan in II, 4, when she
remarks that she does not care that her father will go out into
the storm, become pregnant: "O, sir, to wilful men,/ The
injuries that they themselves procure/ Must be their school-
masters." Regan is, of course, correct, for Lear does learn
from his injuries and suffering. In the figure of Tom, Lear's
injuries seem to take on a physical embodiment, so that Tom
literally becomes Lear's schoolmaster. It is only because he
has learned from his teacher about man's animality that Lear
could utter what is Shakespeare's most cynical speech.

> When I do stare, see how the subject quakes.
> I pardon that man's life. What was thy cause?
> Adultery?
> Thou shalt not die: die for adultery! No:
> The wren goes to 't, and the small gilded fly
> Does lecher in my sight.

Let copulation thrive; for Gloucester's bastard son
Was kinder to his father than my daughters
Got 'tween lawful sheets.
To 't, luxury, pell-mell! for I lack soldiers.
Behold yond simpering dame,
Whose face between her forks presages snow:
That minces virtue, and does shake the head
To hear of pleasure's name;
The fitchew, nor the soiled horse, goes to 't
With a more riotous appetite.
Down from the waist they are Centaurs,
Though women all above:
But to the girdle do the gods inherit,
Beneath is all the fiends';
There's hell, there's darkness, there's the sulphurous pit,
Burning, scalding, stench, consumption; fie, fie, fie! pah,
pah! Give me an ounce of civet, good apothecary, to sweeten
my imagination: there's money for thee.

                              (IV,6,110-34)

Lear's contact with the lowest member of the underworld
gives him an understanding of the human situation that he
never had before. He looks at Tom and sees himself—and
finally sees the only "truth" that the once-proud king could
see. Tom o' Bedlam helps to cure Lear of his blindness in a
play filled with people who cannot see, with or without eyes.

However, Edgar's disguise does double duty, for Edgar
himself needs to be educated. He, like Lear, becomes an
exile in a world that is more cruel than he realizes. In the
play's beginning he is a simple-minded cony; at the end he
is called upon to restore order to the state. He learns about
life, "the thing itself," not only by observing the suffering
of others, especially Lear's, but by the very fact of his existence as a Tom o' Bedlam:

Yet better thus, and known to be contemn'd,
Than still contemn'd and flatter'd. To be worst,
The lowest and most dejected thing of fortune,
Stands still in esperance, lives not in fear;
The lamentable change is from the best;
The worst returns to laughter. Welcome, then,
Thou unsubstantial air that I embrace!
The wretch that thou hast blown unto the worst
Owes nothing to thy blasts.

(IV,1,1-9)

His disguise as Tom has caused him to live as unaccommodated
man, and this has made him truly philosophical. The man
who says "Ripeness is all" is not the same man who unwit-
tingly ran away from his evil brother. He confronted the
world of darkness as a naked wretch, and from this night
he has learned to understand the very stars his brother so
vehemently rejected. The underworld, in the form of a
Falstaff, helped teach Hal to be a better king; so too, in
the mad groans and nakedness of a Bedlam, it teaches
Edgar, as it taught Lear, to see clearly on a darkling heath.

In the disguise of Edgar as Tom o' Bedlam Shakespeare
has used the underworld for symbolic purposes. Poor Tom is
the lowest of the underworld, and therefore the lowest of men
in the order of nature. The disguise allows Edgar to represent a visual symbol of man's bestiality, a symbol which
greatly affects Lear in his madness. In *Timon of Athens*
Shakespeare uses the underworld not as symbolic disguise,
but as symbolic character. As despair deepens in his presentation of tragedy, the image of the underworld seems to
become more defined in symbolic terms.

In the extreme misanthropy of Timon of Athens the underworld is both condemned and used. It is a source of hatred
and the vehicle by which he can spew his disgust on the

world he rejects. The first significant expression of Timon's misanthropy is presented when he is outside the walls of Athens giving his special brand of advice to the mankind within. It includes the following:

> . . . to general filths
> Convert o' the instant, green virginity,
> Do 't in your parents' eyes!

> . . . bound servants, steal!

> Maid, to thy master's bed;
> Thy mistress is o' the brothel!
> (IV,1,6-8;10;12-13)

In a speech which contains the phrase "let confusion thrive!", reference is made to whores ("general filths"), thieving, and the brothel. The underworld comes easily to Timon's lips when he separates himself from the ethics of humanity.

Two scenes later the underworld enters the play in the shape of two whores and Banditti. But before they enter, in another extended piece of invective, Timon utters a comment which explains his behavior to the underworld.

> . . . for every grise of fortune
> Is smooth'd by that below: the learned pate
> Ducks to the golden fool: all's obliquy;
> There 's nothing level in our cursed natures,
> But direct villainy.
> (IV,3,16-20)

This is the misanthropic view of the ethical ladder. The "all's obliquy" takes on all the force of an ethical pronouncement.

The only thing that is "level" is *direct* villainy—that is, a
villainy at least "honest," straightforward, unflattering. To
Timon's disillusioned mind, the whores and thieves are at
least direct in their villainy, far different from the flatterers
who absorbed his wealth like sponges.

He then finds gold, to which he addresses himself:

> Come damned earth,
> Thou common whore of mankind, that put'st odds
> Among the rout of nations, I will make thee
> Do thy right nature.
>
> (IV,3,41-44)

Here the gold is called a whore; its right nature will be to
corrupt mankind. Immediately, the play's two whores enter
in the company of Alcibiades. From the time that Phrynia
and Timandra appear to the time they leave, they serve as
symbols of lust and disease, without losing their realism. Timon
tells Alcibiades: 'This fell whore of thine/ Hath in her
more destruction than the sword." The first words that come
from Phrynia's mouth are: "Thy lips rot off!" Timon answers with "I will not kiss thee; then the rot returns/ To thine
own lips again." He gives Timandra advice:

> Be a whore still. They love thee not that use thee;
> Give them diseases, leaving with thee their lust.
> Make use of thy salt hours; season the slaves
> For tubs and baths; bring down rose-cheek'd youth
> To the tub-fast and the diet.
>
> (IV,3,82-86)

He wants her to infect the mankind he hates. Timon gives
the whores gold, together with advice and curses.

Consumption sow
In hollow bones of man; strike their sharp shins,
And mar men's spurring. Crack the lawyer's voice,
That he may never more false title plead,
Nor sound his quillets shrilly; hoar the flamen,
That scolds against the quality of flesh
And not believes himself. Down with the nose,
Down with it flat; take the bridge quite away
Of him that, his particular to foresee,
Smells from the general weal. Make curl'd-pate ruffians bald;
And let the unscarr'd braggarts of the war
Derive some pain from you. Plague all,
That your activity may defeat and quell
The source of all erection. There's more gold;
Do you damn others, and let this damn you,
And ditches grave you all!

(IV,3,151-66)

This tirade displays Timon's complete hatred of man and his sick desire for the corruption of all mankind. He is hoping that the whores do to men what he would like to do. That is why he wants them to "be strong in whore."

In the same scene three Banditti appear. Timon gives them gold also, and tells them to do villainy. He then presents these important lines:

I'll example you with thievery:
The sun 's a thief, and with his great attraction
Robs the vast sea; the moon 's an arrant thief,
And her pale fire she snatches from the sun:
The sea 's a thief, whose liquid surge resolves
The moon into salt tears: the earth's a thief:
That feeds and breeds by a composture stolen
From general excrement: each thing 's a thief:
The laws, your curb and whip, in their rough power

Have uncheck'd theft. Love not yourselves: away,
Rob one another. There's more gold. Cut throats:
All that you meet are thieves: to Athens go,
Break open shops; nothing can you steal,
But thieves do lose it: steal no less for this
I give you; and gold confound you howsoe'er!
Amen!

(IV,3,438-53)

Timon, his values perverted, sees only injustice in the world. He has surpassed those writers of cony-catching pamphlets who show how common thievery is; he has gone one step further than John Taylor who defended thievery because it was practiced by all members of society. Timon's misanthropy is expressed in terms of thief imagery, but it involves nothing less than the universe.

The play's underworld characters represent direct villainy, and they are called upon by Timon to destroy indirect villainy, that is, the rest of the world. The whores and thieves are symbols of disease and lawlessness; they provide Timon with the texts for his poetical venom. This is no insignificant task, for the play contains little more than the emotional outbursts of a disillusioned and deluded mind.

In the four plays discussed, all tragedies written between 1600 and 1607, Shakespeare has increasingly concentrated on the underworld as a symbol of evil. In this respect he is conforming to the popular dramatic tradition, seen in the moralities and Dekker. However, he gives the traditional image added significance, not only because his art has placed the image in an effective dramatic context, but because the image seems to take on the force of a philosophical statement when it is considered in connection with the idea of final reconciliation found in all Shakespearean tragedy. Is it merely coincidence that those called upon to restore order and health to society, and by extension to the world, in *Othello, King Lear,* and *Timon of Athens* are those who had intimate contact with the underworld? Cassio is called upon to set things right—the man who had as his mistress the whore Bianca. Edgar is asked to rule and sustain the "gor'd state"—the man who *was* an underworld character in his disguise as Tom o' Bedlam. Alcibiades will bring peace and justice to Athens —the man who was accompanied by two rotten whores. In the last case especially, Shakespeare need not have presented Alcibiades in the company of whores. They could have served their symbolic function had they come upon Timon without Alcibiades, as did the Banditti. Surely, the appearance of Alcibiades in the company of two diseased wenches would tend to lower him in the audience's estimation. Surely, Shakespeare realized this. Yet, Shakespeare does present Alcibiades *with* the whores, which leads one to suspect that Alcibiades must know the whores in order to rule successfully. Is knowledge of the underworld through contact necessary for the proper understanding of the basic moral premises by which all men must live, and is not such knowledge necessary for those who wish to rule a state on principles of justice and love? *Othello, Lear,* and *Timon* seem to indicate this, as does *Henry IV,* where Hal studied his underworld companions. For Shakespeare the underworld seem to be the fruit on the forbidden tree; it must be chewed for the proper knowledge of good and evil.

III

As Shakespeare progresses in his development he concentrates more on symbol and allegory. Edgar, as Tom o' Bedlam, is a perfect example of a character whose most important function is symbolic. So too the whores in *Timon of Athens.*

Shakespeare's mind and art worked toward allegory and a symbolic interpretation of the universe. Even his early work seems to be verging on allegory.

In *3 Henry VI* Shakespeare accentuates the horrors of civil war by bringing on stage in a formal artificial way a Son who has killed his Father and a Father who has killed his Son. It is a "piteous spectacle," as Henry VI exclaims, and it emphasizes how "bloody" and "heavy" the times are. The Father and Son have no names; they clearly represent types, as in the morality plays. And they move in the realm of allegory. The unnatural butchery presents a symbolic picture of chaos in the commonwealth. The Son's exclamation, "Pardon me, God, I knew not what I did!" echoes Christ's words on the cross, and point up Shakespeare's belief that the civil war involved terrible waste.

Later in his career, also in the context of civil war, Shakespeare presents a morality play of greater scope played out by characters that are rich and developed. The *Henry IV* plays, as has been suggested earlier in the chapter, can be considered a dramatization of the education of a Prince-Everyman who must choose in morality fashion between Disorder and Rule, or Sloth and Chivalry, or Dishonor and Honor. In this large allegorical context particular elements in the plot take on symbolic significance. For example, the stabbing of the dead Hotspur by Falstaff not only puts Falstaff in his proper moral position, thereby preparing for his rejection by Henry V, but broadens out to signify the victory of Flesh over Spirit, of Dishonor over Exaggerated Honor, and so much more.

In the realm of comedy, and closer to this study of the underworld, Dogberry's bumbling antics and slaughter of the language in *Much Ado About Nothing* also seem to move into allegory. His instructions to the watch are a source of

comedy; they lead the audience to expect no results from
the inept crew which is told by Dogberry to "comprehend
all vagrom men." Indeed, his instructions stress comprehension rather than apprehension:

> If you meet a thief, you must suspect him, by virtue of
> your office, to be no true man; and, for such kind of
> men, the less you meddle or make with them, why, the
> more is for your honesty.

WATCH: If we know him to be a thief, shall we not lay hands
on him?

DOG: Truly, by your office, you may; but I think they that
touch pitch will be defiled: the most peaceable way
for you, if you do take a thief, is to let him show himself what he is and steal out of your company.

(III,3,52-63)

And yet, Dogberry brings to light in his own meandering
verbalizing way what no one else in the play could. Only
in a comic world could such a constable as Dogberry function, and only in a comedy could his watch apprehend the
villains of the play. But his presence points to larger issues.
Much Ado is based on the theme of deception—of others and
self. Dogberry, although he suffers from the delusions of vanity, manifested by his erratic verbosity, gropes to success. He
instinctively distrusts Borachio: "I do not like thy look, I
promise thee." And he has a proper set of values, although
comically stated: "Write down, that they hope they serve
God: and write God first; for God defend but God should
go before such villains!" His presence is an effective contrast
to the villainy and more serious deceit in the play. Essentially,
he softens the villainy. His suggestion that the watch allow a
thief to steal out of its company causes Verges to call him
a "merciful man." Indeed, the idea of mercy causes the

villainy in the plot to become overshadowed by the gay, for-
giving world of the play. In this connection even Dogberry's
malapropisms are operating. He angrily tells Conrade: "O
villain! thou wilt be condemned into everlasting redemption
for this." The wrong word "redemption" highlights the mercy
idea, and in the association of mercy with thieves calls to
mind the forgiveness of the thief on the cross by Christ.
Dogberry, therefore, contributes to the underlying mood of
the play, and suggests issues that go beyond the mere relationship of a constable to his watch and his vocation of
catching thieves.

The Elizabethans understood allegory and were conditioned
to it, as Chapter 2 has demonstrated. Shakespeare's allegorical
sense becomes definite and pervasive, however, in *Measure for
Measure,* where the lechery in Vienna becomes lechery in the
world. Shakespeare's treatment of the underworld in *Measure*
gives a revealing indication of his development.

Just as the taverns of the morality plays assumed the entire
world of sin, so the stews of Vienna in *Measure* assume the
entire world. Shakespeare is presenting a far-reaching Christian drama, using Vienna as a moral focus and the underworld as the focusing instrument. The play is filled with
"traders in the flesh," from the lowly Mistress Overdone to
the high Angelo. The atmosphere of the stew envelops Vienna.
The underworld is so pervasive a world in this play and it so
meaningfully interacts with the world of official Vienna that
the city seems to be one gigantic diseased brothel.

The overlapping between the underworld and the official
world begins in I,2. Lucio is speaking to two gentlemen about
diseases. When the bawd Mistress Overdone enters, Lucio
exclaims, "Behold, behold, where Madam Mitigation comes!"
He says that he purchased many diseases under her roof.
After more talk of disease, Mistress Overdone tells the others

that Claudio has been arrested. This important piece of business with which official Vienna is concerned is related first by an important member of the play's underworld. When she is left alone she laments that her brothel is getting very few customers. Pompey, her servant, enters to report more dire news to her: "All houses in the suburbs of Vienna must be plucked down." After learning about the new enforcement of laws in Vienna, she states: "Why, here's a change indeed in the commonwealth! What shall become of me?" The comment is interesting. The play's bawd allies the state affairs with her own affairs. This strong overlapping between state and underworld continues throughout the play, with the result that the underworld and the overworld become one— and this one world is morally diseased.

The official hand of the law affects the underworld when Elbow the constable enters with Pompey and Froth in II,1. They have been arrested for having been found in a "common" house, Froth as a visitor, Pompey as a "parcel-bawd; one that serves a bad woman." Elbow is, like Dogberry, a misuser of words whose malapropisms are pregnant: "First, an it like you, the house is a respected house; next, this is a respected fellow; and his mistress is a respected woman." In the disordered world of the play the malapropism is functioning because those "two notorious benefactors" who are suspected of ill fame are respected. When Escalus asks Pompey, "How would you live, Pompey? by being a bawd? What do you think of the trade, Pompey? is it a lawful trade?", Pompey presents this interesting answer: "If the law would allow it, sir." Pompey, in his own cynical way, sees to the heart of the matter in a world where morality is changeable. Escalus warns Pompey that he will get a whipping if caught again, and allows him to leave. This points up the perversion of the law in Vienna, where Justice will kill a man for fornication and Mercy lets a bawd go free.

In III,2 Elbow brings in Pompey again. The disguised Duke asks Elbow what Pompey's offense is. Elbow says: "Marry, sir, he hath offended the law: and, sir, we take him to be a thief too, sir." The *too* is enlightening, for is not a thief an offender? The remark indicates Elbow's foolishness, but it also suggests that only sexual offenses are true offenses in the rotten state of Vienna. The Duke ignores the thief reference, but readily picks up the bawd idea.

> Fie, sirrah! a bawd, a wicked bawd!
> The evil that thou causest to be done,
> That is thy means to live. Do thou but think
> What 'tis to cram a maw or clothe a back
> From such a filthy vice: say to thyself,
> From their abominable and beastly touches
> I drink, I eat, array myself, and live.
> Canst thou believe thy living is a life,
> So stinkingly depending? Go mend, go mend.
>   (III,2,20-28)

The Duke then calls Pompey a rude beast, a Dekkerian epithet for members of the underworld, and tells the officer to take him to prison. Before Pompey leaves, however, Lucio enters and they exchange a few words on Mistress Overdone, venereal disease, whores and bawds. The whore idea lingers in Lucio's mind when he tells the disguised Duke about the Duke's lechery: "The Duke, I say to thee again, would eat mutton on Fridays. He's not past it yet, and I say to thee, he would mouth with a beggar, though she smelt brown bread and garlic: say that I said so" (III,2,191-95). Lucio will regret this statement later, but it can be seen that even the Duke gathers to himself some of the Vienna atmosphere in the foul mind of Lucio. Mistress Overdone then makes her last appearance, on her way to being punished. Lucio, it

seems, informed against her. "My lord," she says, "this is
one Lucio's information against me. Mistress Kate Keepdown was with child by him in the Duke's time; he promised
her marriage: his child is a year and a quarter old, come
Philip and Jacob: I have kept it myself: and see how he
goes about to abuse me" (III,2,210-15). Her words indicate
a kindheartedness on the part of the bawd, a quality that
is difficult to find in most of the play's characters.

The underworld-state relationship is intensified when Pompey is asked to be executioner's assistant. Abhorson is per-
turbed to learn that a bawd will be his assistant—"A bawd,
sir? fie upon him! He will discredit our mystery" (IV,2,30).
But Pompey convinces him that his own profession is also
a mystery. A member of the underworld thereby becomes
an official member of the state. The overlapping becomes
even more obvious when Pompey compares his new job to
his old one: "I am as well acquainted here as I was in our
house of profession: one would think it were Mistress
Overdone's own house, for here be many of her old customers" (IV,3,1-5). Shakespeare had often referred to the
world as a prison, but here the world is a prison and a
brothel. Pompey's comparison is effective and devastating.

In the last act the Duke sums up his impressions of
Vienna.

> My business in this state
> Made me a looker on here in Vienna
> Where I have seen corruption boil and bubble
> Till it o'er-run the stew; laws for all faults,
> But faults so countenanced, that the strong statutes
> Stand like the forfeits in a barber's shop,
> As much in mock as mark.
>
> (V,1,318-24)

The stew reference has its double meaning. The corruption that the Duke observed makes him feel that all of Vienna is a stew, an idea presented throughout the play. The Duke is, as some critics assert,[10] a Christ figure who disguises himself in order to cleanse the corruption of Vienna. The Christian story, with its distinctly Christian theme of Justice vs. Mercy, expands Vienna to the world and expands the underworld to all the physical and moral corruption in the world. The disease and stench of the stew overruns the world until a Christ causes the boiling and bubbling of corruption to cease. He does this by dispensing true Justice. It is fitting that the Duke punish Lucio by forcing him to marry a whore, Mistress Kate Keepdown—"Marrying a punk, my lord, is pressing to death, whipping, and hanging." It is also fitting that the Duke should defer the execution of Barnardine, who has not repented for his sins. The Duke, in showing mercy to Barnardine, strongly suggests Christ pardoning the thief on the cross. The underworld is the object of both acts of mercy and becomes the fabric of a recurrent Christian idea. That Mercy and the underworld have a strong bond is best accentuated, in another connection, when Isabella, disgusted with Claudio's reaction to Angelo's proposition to her, utters:

> Thy sin's not accidental, but a trade.
> Mercy to thee would prove itself a bawd:
> 'Tis best thou diest quickly.
>   (III,1,149-51)

Since Justice contends with Mercy within the atmosphere of a diseased world, it is not surprising for Isabella to ally Mercy with a bawd. She has already been tempted by Angelo, who is acting as chief authority of the stew-state and to whom, as the audience has overheard, the idea of whore comes naturally when he becomes infatuated with Isabella.

. . . never could the strumpet
With all her double vigour, art and nature,
Once stir my temper; but this virtuous maid
Subdues me quite.

(II,2,183-86)

When the world is a stew even the "ensky'd and sainted"
Isabella will think of Mercy in connection with a bawd and
will be contrasted to a strumpet.

The underworld is an essential part of the moral and artistic
framework of *Measure for Measure.* Shakespeare relentlessly
fuses the underworld with the overworld. The fortunes of
Mistress Overdone overlap with the fortunes of the state.
Pompey acquires an official job. Disease infects brothel and
state. The Justice-Mercy theme is presented within a brothel
atmosphere which envelops the world. Yet, Shakespeare's
treatment of the underworld is not completely unsympathetic.
Pompey has a natural honesty that is lacking in most of the
other characters, and Mistress Overdone, in caring for Lucio's
child, performs a genuine act of kindness. These two characters do have the taints of their vocations; yet, when *all* of
Vienna is a brothel, the bawd and her accomplice cannot be
considered more evil than any of the other tainted characters.
In contrast to Angelo and Lucio, they seem "honest." The
very underworld which reflects the corruption of the world
has within it some of the qualities that redeem mankind.
Shakespeare has given the traditional double image a new
dimension. He has allowed the underworld to assume the
world, but has not drained the human sediment of all its
humanity.

In *Measure for Measure* a Christian cosmic drama is played
out in a brothel world. When Shakespeare next uses the
brothel as a moral focus, in *Pericles,* he places it in a pagan

world, but retains a distinctly religious sense and makes the brothel emblematic of evil and sin. The underworld once again has an allegorical function, as it does in the moralities, and the fortunes of Marina represent the fortunes of Innocence in a world of sin. The brothel becomes the testing-ground of virtue in *Pericles,* just as the governor of the brothel world of *Measure for Measure* was a test of virtue for Isabella.

If *Pericles* has a main theme, it centers on the fortunes of the lost Marina. Her stay in the brothel is the most revealing and interesting challenge this pure maiden must face. The assertion by Bertrand Evans that until Marina's ordeal in the brothel "no person (in the play) has tried to master his fate" [11] points up the importance of the brothel scenes. Marina is sold by pirates to Pandar and Bawd, who happily buy her, for virgins are rare in their brothel. In fact, they complain that their prostitutes are "rotten"—one "poor Transylvanian" has already been made "roast meat for worms" because of one of the girls. Now that Marina will be with them, they believe business will be better. Boult is told to spread the news of her arrival. Marina laments that she was not killed by Leonine or thrown overboard by the pirates. The Bawd, to console her, tells her that she "shall live in pleasure," that she shall "taste gentlemen of all fashions." Marina stops her ears, but not her mouth. "Are you a woman?" she asks the Bawd. It is the kind of question Desdemona would ask, and indicates how difficult it is for Innocence to understand Evil. Boult returns to tell of future customers, all anxious to see the new acquisition. The last words of Marina in this first brothel scene are: "If fires be hot, knives sharp, or waters deep,/ Untied I still my virgin knot will keep./ Diana, aid my purpose!" (IV,2,159-61). The Bawd wonders, "What have we to do with Diana?" *We* have nothing to do with Diana, but Marina's relationship with Diana is a close one. She is a chaste virgin, and her mother is one of Diana's priestesses.

Marina's activities in the brothel are discussed before they are witnessed. Two gentlemen, talking on the street in front of the brothel, express their surprise at having found "divinity preached" in a brothel. They will frequent no more brothels; instead they will "go hear vestals sing." Having heard the pure Marina preach, they are prepared for the vestals. The spirit of Diana lurks in a brothel.

The play's long brothel scene begins with Pandar, Bawd, and Boult complaining of Marina's actions—"she would make a puritan of the devil." Then Lord Lysimachus enters, disguised, but they recognize him. He seems to be an experienced frequenter of brothels: "How now! wholesome iniquity have you that a man may deal withal, and defy the surgeon?" (IV,6, 28-29). The reason for his presence in the brothel is somewhat ambiguous. His preliminary conversation indicates that he came to the brothel to obtain a whore. And when he first speaks with Marina, he seems anxious to sleep with her— "Come, bring me to some private place: come, come." But her little speech in which she talks of this "sty" where diseases are sold, causes him to profess his role as observer rather than participator—"Had I brought hither a corrupted mind,/ Thy speech had alter'd it." This is a more proper role for the man who will become Marina's husband. He calls Marina "a piece of virtue," proclaims a curse on whoever robs her of her "goodness," and leaves, calling Boult a "damned door-keeper." All of this is, of course, perturbing to the keepers of the brothel, because Marina makes their profession "stink afore the face of the gods." The Bawds asks her: "Will you not go the way of woman-kind?"—a question that a Hamlet, Lear, or Timon would ask in bitterness. But Marina is a

woman of a different world. She is left by the Bawd to be
deflowered by Boult, but her words once again save her virginity. When Boult asks her, and the question itself shows Marina's power, "What would you have me do?", she presents this
strong utterance:

> Do any thing but this thou doest. Empty
> Old receptacles, or common shores of filth;
> Serve by indenture to the common hangman:
> Any of these are yet better than this;
> For what thou professest, a baboon, could he speak,
> Would own a name too dear.
>
> (IV,6,185-90)

By the time the scene ends she not only keeps her virtue, but
convinces Boult that she does not belong in a brothel. Gower,
in the Prologue to Act V, informs the audience that "Marina
thus the brothel 'scapes."

The clash between Marina and the brothel is nothing less
than the confrontation of Innocence and Evil. It takes on
the proportions of a moral drama, in which Innocence and
Chastity are able to defeat Evil and Sin. The brothel, traditionally—and in this play realistically—connected with sin
and disease and filth, accentuates the purity of Marina. That
this purity has great strength is indicated by the reactions of
the two gentlemen, Lysimachus, and Boult. Just as a saint
becomes truly known in adversity, so the purity of Marina
becomes known when she is tested in an underworld situation.
Light is known because of dark.

The challenge of the brothel to Marina becomes especially
appropriate when the importance of the goddess Diana is
recognized. Marina calls on Diana for aid. Marina's mother
is a priestess of Diana. And Diana herself appears to Pericles
in a vision and at the end of the play to set everything right.

What, therefore, could be more appropriate than to have Marina, a model of chastity and a true daughter of Diana, clash with a brothel—and win her battle?

Shakespeare, therefore, not only makes the underworld emblematic of sin and corruption, but also uses it as an effective instrument for testing virgin innocence, as *Measure for Measure* and *Pericles* demonstrate. The idea of a virgin in peril is also found in his last play, *The Tempest,* in the relationship between Miranda and Caliban. Of course, Caliban is not an underworld character, although he, like the members of the underworld, symbolically represents a lower order of being. The Dekkerian "beasts" of the underworld have some echoes in that "beast Caliban," as Prospero calls him. Also, Miranda's virtue is not tested, as is Isabella's and Marina's, for Caliban's attempted rape of Miranda was stopped by Prospero. In the brave old world of Prospero's isle, Miranda operates as a pawn and therefore has little capacity to act. But Miranda's danger because of a Caliban on the island seems to be part of a pattern of Shakespeare's thought which likes to play on the idea of virgin innocence dropped into an underworld situation. Caliban, like the underworld, is both emblematic and real. He is vivid in dramatic terms and representational in allegorical terms. His attempted seduction of Miranda is an extension of Angelo's of Isabella and the brothel's of Marina. In each case, the woman is a symbol of Virtue and cannot be contaminated by the representative of sin and evil. In each case, the underworld, or a shade of the underworld, serves as a revealing moral focus.

IV

Using the underworld as a reflector, as an image, and as a moral focus, Shakespeare has transformed a traditional idea into an exciting dramatic instrument. He has taken a world that is part of his cultural milieu and enriched it by artistically reinterpreting it. His attitude toward the underworld is somewhat similar to the attitude of Dekker. The underworld is a danger to society; it is an evil world. When disorder is an issue in the history plays, Shakespeare uses the underworld to reveal this disorder. When he wishes to indicate that a world is corrupt and diseased, he uses the underworld as a reflection of this world. His prostitutes are diseased; his brothels overflow with corruption; his thieves steal their way to the gallows. He, like Dekker, reflects the climate of opinion surrounding the underworld, although his ability to make some of his underworld characters warmly human often seems to soften the evil side of that opinion. But, his artistic treatment of the underworld is vastly different from Dekker's. In the Falstaff plays, the underworld becomes a structural entity that significantly reflects the political world. In *Hamlet, Othello, King Lear,* and *Timon of Athens* the underworld operates as a vivid image which develops into a rich symbol. In *Measure for Measure* and *Pericles* it serves as a moral focus and finds its place in the allegorical worlds of these plays.

Shakespeare, like Jonson, fully capitalized on the potentialities of the underworld as a dramatic component. For the underworld, by its very nature, could serve both realism and allegory, as it did in the morality plays. At the same time, the attitude toward the underworld was richly ambiguous, for the same world that was sinful and disorderly could be humorous. Whereas Dekker usually presented the underworld as evil, without humour, and treated the underworld realistically without extending its function to comment on life in symbolic terms, Shakespeare played on all aspects of the base string in the course of his development. Autolycus, the marvelous rogue of *The Winter's Tale,* coming toward the end of his career, vividly demonstrates Shakespeare's many uses of the underworld.

Just as the realistic underworld of the brothel entered the romance *Pericles,* so too the realistic underworld of Autolycus enters *The Winter's Tale.* Autolycus makes his first appearance, in this tale of sin and redemption, singing a ditty about his life as a rogue. He mentions white sheets on hedges, quarts of ale, tumbling in the hay, and the possibility of the stocks in the future. He interrupts his song with this piece of information: "I have served Prince Florizel and in my time wore three-pile; but now I am out of service." Being out of service has caused many an Elizabethan rogue to tramp the roads. He explains that his "traffic is sheets; . . . Gallows and knock are too powerful on the highway: beating and hanging are terrors to me: for the life to come, I sleep out the thought of it" (IV,3,28-31). When the Clown enters, Autolycus drops to the ground, moans that he has been robbed, and picks the Clown's pocket as he is being helped up. Autolycus tells the Clown that he was robbed by that Autolycus who "having flown over many knavish professions . . . settled on rogue." The Clown knows Autolycus' reputation, for he says: "Out upon him! prig, for my life, prig: he haunts wakes, fairs and bear-baitings." When the Clown departs, Autolycus announces that he will be going to the sheep-shearing. He leaves the stage singing.

The first appearance of Autolycus shows him to be a typical Elizabethan rogue roaming the roads of Bohemia. His onstage pickpocketing of the Clown is merely a dramatized rogue-pamphlet incident. Autolycus is filled with the merry rogue spirit; his singing and his attitude typify the romantic side of roguery.

Autolycus enters again in the famous pastoral scene (IV,4),

filled with flowers and dances, the young love of Perdita and Florizel, and the watchfulness of the disguised older men. He brings with him assorted trifles, including ballads. He sings his wares, peddles his items, and adds to the general festivities. But he is no mere peddler, for an Elizabethan rogue takes advantage of every opportunity to steal. While he sold his trumpery, he relates, he saw "whose purse was best in picture; and what I saw, to my good use I remembered." When all the buyers gathered round him, he went to work: "So that in this time of lethargy I picked and cut most of their festival purses."

He is asked to exchange clothes with Florizel, so that the prince can leave Bohemia undetected. When he is alone he states:

I understand the business, I hear it: to have an open ear, a quick eye, and a nimble hand, is necessary for a cutpurse; . . . I see this is the time that the unjust man doth thrive. What an exchange had this been without boot! What a boot is here with this exchange! Sure the gods do this year connive at us, and we may do anything extempore. The prince himself is about a piece of iniquity, stealing away from his father with his clog at his heels.

(IV,4,683-98)

And when he sees the Shepherd and the Clown he says:

Aside, aside; here is more matter for a hot brain: every lane's end, every shop, church, session, hanging, yields a careful man work.

(IV,4,699-701)

Autolycus has the attributes of the pickpocket, and he knows where to find his prey. He is also, as the previous scene demonstrated, a rogue that walks the roads to find sheets. Shakespeare combines the city and the country underworlds in the person of the one Autolycus.

Autolycus then poses as a courtier in his newly acquired clothes, and thereby learns that Perdita is not the Shepherd's daughter. He feels that Fortune is with him, and he, with the Shepherd and Clown, will reveal what he has learned to the king. He believes that this affair may advance him again in court favor. In his pose as a courtier there is a falling off in the audience's attitude toward Autolycus. G. Wilson Knight's observation that Autolycus is "being used to elaborate the vein of court satire" and that "after donning courtier's clothes, his humour takes an unnecessarily cruel turn" [12] correctly accentuates the reason for Autolycus' fall. And Knight's comparison of Autolycus to Falstaff is equally pertinent. For both rogues become less humorous as the scenes of their respective plays progress, and both must of necessity be rejected—Falstaff by Hal, Autolycus by an audience that has switched its attention and sympathy to the Clown. It is fitting, therefore, that Autolycus asks the Clown to pardon him for his faults at the end of the play.

With no intention of doing good for anyone but himself, Autolycus does good in the course of things. It is through his machinations that the Perdita plot is brought to a successful conclusion. He tricks Shepherd and Clown into going aboard the prince's ship and they eventually reveal the true history of Perdita. In this respect he acts as an instrument of the gods. His very name suggests that this earthy rogue somehow is connected with higher forces, and his own statement seems to verify this: "If I had a mind to be honest I see Fortune would not suffer me: she drops booties in my mouth." His own plans go awry, but he becomes the unwitting, and perhaps inevitable, instrument for good. Either the gods work through all kinds of people, even rogues, or this particular rogue is surrounded by a vague godliness.

Shakespeare brings Autolycus into the world of Bohemia because he is, for the most part, a source of fun and good humour. He is a colorful rogue, who adds to the play's color and music. He also has the dramatic function of bringing the Perdita plot to a successful conclusion. But this is not all. The diversity of moods and characters in *The Winter's Tale* is a key to another aspect of his role. The play is filled with the high and the low, with birth and death and rebirth. In this scheme Autolycus, like the disguised Edgar in *King Lear,* is the representative of the lowest, the underworld, and he takes what he can from life. In a sense, he, despite his obvious jollity and the pride he has in his abilities as thief, would like to be reborn in the prince's service. But he cannot. He must continue to walk the roads of Bohemia, looking for sheets and crowds. Of course, the audience feels no sadness about his plight, because he *is* a rogue, because his spirit is essentially merry, and because the audience is not sympathetic toward him at the play's end. Shakespeare casts no moral opinion against him; obviously, the play can hold no such opinion. It seems enough that the gods can work through the most roguish rogue in the plays of Shakespeare. He is the lowest member of the world of *The Winter's Tale* and, in some strange way, he acts in behalf of the highest.

But this too is not all. For Autolycus gives to the world of the pastoral, with its symbolism and its great issues of life and death, a sense of reality. He allows the pastoral to touch the earth in a realistic way. Autolycus enters the play in the scene immediately preceding the famous pastoral scene to sing of daffodils and hedges. But these are placed in a far different context than the flowers talked about by Perdita and Florizel. They belong to a different world, but a world that must be included in the large issues of the play. Autolycus then

enters the colorful sheep-shearing scene with all of his everyday cunning—a cunning recognizable to every Elizabethan
in the audience. In a play where the gods are at work,
Shakespeare, by means of the underworld's representative,
Autolycus, introduces a world that his audience knows first-
hand. The writers of the morality plays had similarly brought
in the underworld in order to have their allegories touch everyday life. The underworld, in short, plants Shakespeare's winter's tale on earth—and one is forced to remember that it
is the same earth for Perdita and Autolycus. Whereas the
former looks at the earth for flowers of spring, the latter
looks for sheets. And the gods look at both.

Shakespeare's treatment of the underworld in each play
discussed gives an indication of the quality of his mind and
art. He uses the idea of whore to make his audience better
understand a Hamlet and an Othello. He transplants a Tom
o' Bedlam from the roads of Elizabethan England to the dark
mad world of *King Lear,* and makes that Bedlam serve as a
philosopher. He transplants another Elizabethan rogue to a
pastoral Bohemia and allows him to become an instrument
of the gods. He gives to a fat highwayman a humanity that
is deep and penetrating. He reflects political disorder in the
robbery of a franklin. He causes a city and a brothel to inter-
act so meaningfully that they become one. He tests virgin
innocence by dropping it into an underworld situation.

The underworld was part of the London that Shakespeare
and his audience knew so well. Shakespeare uses that underworld as a revealing reflector, image, and moral focus, and
thereby makes it a vehicle for an art that goes far beyond
the confines of place or time.

Conclusion

The uses of the underworld by Dekker, Jonson, and Shakespeare show them to be men whose assumptions about the underworld were shaped by the contemporary climate of opinion surrounding it and intensified by the image of the underworld provided by the morality tradition. To be aware of this is, of course, only the beginning of a critical evaluation of these dramatists, but it is an important beginning. The audience came to the theater with a set of opinions and expectations, about the underworld and almost everything else. The dramatists played upon these expectations. Dekker accepts and usually transmits the conventional image of the underworld. Jonson draws on the popular image, but refines it and sometimes inverts it to suit his satiric and dramatic purpose. Shakespeare accepts the image, and enriches it by making it a meaningful part of an artistic complex. Their use of the underworld provides a valid commentary on their artistic achievement.

Focusing on the underworld allows one to notice that Jonson, writing his great plays of the middle period, softened his morality, saw the men of his world as neither good nor bad, but as rogues and fools, and used his rogues to mock his fools. On the other hand, most of Dekker's plays are influenced by the pressures of theatrical compromise working on a highly moral personal attitude; they are not informed by an artistic consciousness. Shakespeare's use of the underworld demonstrates his basic concept of character, that both good and bad are mingled in man's nature. His fundamental view of human nature and the traditional image of the underworld, therefore, intensify one another and lead to such magnificent creations as Falstaff and Autolycus. Jonson, it seems, is closer to Shakespeare in being an understanding observer of mankind, while Dekker often shows himself to be more judge than observer.[1]

Dekker, Jonson, and Shakespeare are not the only Elizabethans who sounded the base string. Because it was an active and publicized segment of Elizabethan society, and because it played a pregnant role in the moralities, the underworld is a rich element in Elizabethan drama. The study of its function in the plays of other Elizabethans will, perhaps, shed new light on a particular dramatist's purpose and method; it at least will intensify the light already shining—which surely is an important purpose of scholarship and criticism.

Notes

CHAPTER 1

[1] The following statutes pertain directly or indirectly to rogues and vagabonds. Those in parentheses pertain indirectly. 3 Henry VIII, c.9; (6 Henry VIII, c.3); 22 Henry VIII, c.10, c.12; (25 Henry VIII, c.13); 27 Henry VIII, c.25, (c.28); 28 Henry VIII, c.6; 31 Henry VIII, c.7, (c.13); 33 Henry VIII, c.8, c.14, c.17; 34 Henry VIII & 35 Henry VIII, c.1; 1 Edward VI, c.3, c.12; (2 & 3 Edward VI, c.15); 3 & 4 Edward VI, c.15, c.16; 5 & 6 Edward VI, c.2, c.21; 7 Edward VI, c.11; 1 Mary, stat.2, c. 13; 1 & 2 Philip & Mary, c.4; 2 & 3 Philip & Mary, c.5; 4 & 5 Philip & Mary, c.9; 5 Elizabeth, c.3, c.15, c.16, c.20; 14 Elizabeth, c.5; 18 Elizabeth, c.3; 35 Elizabeth, c.17; 39 Elizabeth, (c.3), c.4, c.17; 43 Elizabeth, c.2, c.3; 1 James I, c.7, c.12, c.25, (c.31); 3 James I, c.21; 7 James I, c.4.

[2] Proclamation of Henry VIII, 26 May 1545. Quoted in *The English Drama and Stage*, 1543–1664, ed. W. C. Hazlitt (London, 1869), p. 6.

[3] Proclamation of Edward VI, 28 April 1551. Quoted in Hazlitt, p. 12.

[4] Statute 14 Elizabeth, c.5 (1571-2).

[5] *Acts of the Privy Council of England*, ed. J. R. Dasent (London, 1905), XXIX, 128.

[6] John Strype, *Annals of the Reformation* (Oxford, 1824), IV, 404.

[7] *Acts*, XXV, 230.

[8] Thomas Platter, *Travels in England, 1599*, trans. Clare Williams (London, 1937), p. 189.

[9] Platter, p. 174.

[10] Platter, p. 174.

[11] Fynes Moryson, *An Itinerary, 1617* (Glasgow, 1907), p. 408.

[12] R. H. Tawney, *The Agrarian Problem in the Sixteenth Century* (London, 1912), p. 268.

[13] William Harrison, *Description of England*, ed. F. J. Furnivall, New Shakespeare Society (London, 1877), p. 218.

[14] Harrison, p. 281.

[15] Arthur Underhill, "Law," in *Shakespeare's England* (Oxford, 1917), I, 398.

[16] W. K. Jordan, *Philanthropy in England* (London, 1959), p. 79. The figure is found in *Stanley's Remedy* (London, 1646).

[17] *Middlesex County Records*, ed. J. C. Jeaffreson (London, 1888-92), I, 67.

[18] *Middlesex*, I, 81.

[19] *Middlesex*, I, 75.

[20] Perhaps the most important reason for vagrancy in England was the displacement of the rural population when pasturage was increased. An excellent discussion of this problem can be found in Tawney, *Agrarian Problem*, pp. 268–80.

[21] Statute 14 Elizabeth, c.5 (1571–2).

[22] A. V. Judges, *Elizabethan Underworld* (London, 1930), p. 492.

[23] Louis B. Wright, *Middle-Class Culture in Elizabethan England* (Chapel Hill, 1935), p. 97.

[24] Thomas Harman, *A Caveat or Warening for Commen Cursetors* (1567), Early English Text Society, eds. Edward Viles and F. J. Furnivall (London, 1869), p. 19.

[25] Harman, p. 28.

[26] Robert Greene, *Thirde and last part of Conny-Catching* (1592), in *The Life and Works of Robert Greene*, ed. A. B. Grosart (London, 1881–86), X, 139.

[27] Harman, p. 21.

[28] Thomas Dekker, *Belman of London* (1608), in Temple Classics (London, 1904), p. 67.

[29] Thomas Middleton, *The Black Booke* (1604), in *The Works of Thomas Middleton*, ed. A. H. Bullen (London, 1886), VIII, 6.

[30] Samuel Rowlands, *Martin Mark-All* (1610), in *The Complete Works of Samuel Rowlands* (Glasgow, 1880), II, 17.

[31] Samuel Rowlands, *Diogines Lanthorne* (London, 1607), C2.

[32] Thomas Dekker, *Lanthorne and Candle-Light* (1608) in Temple Classics (London, 1904), p. 165.

[33] Thomas Nash, *Pierce Penniless's Supplication to the Devil* (1592), Shakespeare Society Reprints, ed. J. P. Collier (London, 1842), p. 64.

[34] Rowlands, *Martin Mark-All*, p. 16.

[35] *Life and Death of Gamaliel Ratsey* (1605), Shakespeare Association Facsimiles, No. 10 (London, 1935), sig. E4.

[36] *Ratseis Ghost* (1605), Shakespeare Association Facsimiles, No. 10 (London, 1935), sig. F2.

[37] *Certain Sermons or Homilies*. Appointed to be Read in Churches, in the Time of Queen Elizabeth of famous Memory (London, 1683), p. 182.

[38] *Certain Sermons or Homilies*, p. 359.

[39] E. M. Leonard, *Early History of English Poor Relief* (Cambridge, 1900), p. 70.

40 Samuel Rid, *The Art of Jugling* (1614), University Microfilms (Ann Arbor), sig. B2.

41 Parson Haben or Hyberdyne, *A Sermon in Praise of Thieves and Thievery* (n.d.), Early English Text Society, eds. Edward Viles and F. J. Furnivall (London, 1869), p. 93.

42 Parson Haben, p. 95.

43 John Taylor, *An Arrant Thief* (London, 1622), A2.

44 Taylor, B8ᵛ.

45 John Taylor, *All the Workes of John Taylor* (London, 1630), p. 93.

46 Carlos Garcia, *The Sonne of the Rogue* (London, 1638), p. 102.

47 Rowlands, *Martin Mark-All,* p. 13.

CHAPTER 2

1 A. C. Cawley, ed. *Everyman and Medieval Miracle Plays* (London, 1956), p. 157.

2 E. K. Chambers, *English Literature at the Close of the Middle Ages* (Oxford, 1945), p. 38.

3 John Speirs, "The Towneley *Shepherds' Plays*" in *The Age of Shakespeare,* ed. Boris Ford (London, 1954), p. 170.

4 William M. Manly, "Shepherds and Prophets: Religious Unity in the Towneley *Secunda Pastorum*," *PMLA,* LXXVIII (June, 1963), 154.

5 E. K. Chambers, *The Medieval Stage* (Oxford, 1903), II, 156.

6 This scheme is discussed in detail in L. W. Cushman, *The Devil and the Vice in the English Dramatic Literature before Shakespeare* (Halle, 1900).

7 The source for all dates in this chapter is Alfred Harbage, *Annals of English Drama* (Philadelphia, 1940).

8 Albert G. Baugh, *A Literary History of England* (New York, 1948), p. 285.

9 Willard Farnham, *The Medieval Heritage of Elizabethan Tragedy* (Berkeley, 1936), p. 197.

10 Bernard Spivack, *Shakespeare and the Allegory of Evil* (New York, 1958), p. 86.

11 The use of the word "interlude" also becomes pronounced. It is a word that has gathered to itself many meanings. For the purposes of this study, it need not be defined. Whether particular plays are interludes with morality elements or moralities with interlude elements, they are still in the morality tradition.

12 Thomas M. Parrott, *Shakespearean Comedy* (New York, 1949), p. 30.

13 Willard Thorp, *The Triumph of Realism in Elizabethan Drama: 1558–1612* (Princeton, 1928), p. 13.

14 C. F. Tucker Brooke, *The Tudor Drama* (New York, 1911), p. 122.

15 A fine discussion of the importance of such comic scenes in the growth of structure in Tudor drama can be found in David M. Bevington, *From Mankind to Marlowe* (Cambridge, Mass., 1962).

16 Spivack, p. 292.

17 W. Roy Mackenzie, *The English Moralities from the Point of View of Allegory* (Boston, 1914), p. ix.

18 That it never dies is convincingly demonstrated by Spivack.

Chapter 3

1 A fine discussion of Dekker as spokesman for his London audience is found in L. C. Knights, *Drama and Society in the Age of Jonson* (London, 1951).

2 Thomas Dekker, *Bel-Man of London* (1608), in Temple Classics (London, 1904), p. 89.

3 Thomas Dekker, *Lanthorne and Candle-Light* (1608), in Temple Classics (London, 1904), p. 165.

4 Thomas Dekker, *O per se O* (1612), in *Elizabethan Underworld* (London, 1930), p. 368.

5 Thomas Dekker, *Old Fortunatus,* Act II, scene 2, 11. 69-72, in *The Dramatic Works of Thomas Dekker,* ed. Fredson Bowers (Cambridge, 1955–61), 4 vols. (Subsequent references will be made to this edition.)

6 *The Whore of Babylon* was entered in the Stationers' Register on 20 April 1607. According to Fredson Bowers, "the speculation has been advanced that the play is a revision of *Truth's Supplication to Candle-light,* for which Henslowe, for the Admiral's men, was paying Dekker in January of 1600" (II,493) although "this is undemonstrable." The play seems to belong to Dekker's early period both in spirit and method and has consequently been placed there for the purposes of this study.

7 Elmer E. Stoll, *John Webster* (Boston, 1905), pp. 45–55.

8 Mary L. Hunt largely attributes this change in Dekker to the influence of Middleton. *Thomas Dekker* (New York, 1911). p. 92.

9 Part I of *The Honest Whore* is essentially Dekker's. Although Middleton may have written one or two scenes, his "part in the play seems to have been relatively minor." (Bowers, II, 14). Dekker's name alone appears on the title page. Part 2 is definitely Dekker's unassisted work.

10 Charles Lamb, *Specimens of English Dramatic Poets* (New York, 1851), p. 65.

11 A. H. Bullen, *Elizabethans* (London, 1925), p. 77.

12 Algernon C. Swinburne, *The Age of Shakespeare* (New York, 1908), p. 67.

13 Frederick E. Pierce, *The Collaboration of Webster and Dekker* (New York, 1909), p. 3.

14 Una Ellis-Fermor, *The Jacobean Drama* (London, 1953), p. 118.

[15] Swinburne, p. 74.

[16] Gamaliel Bradford ("The Women of Dekker," *Sewanee Review*, XXXIII (1925), 290) would not even dismiss it with a chuckle; he considers the underplot "exceedingly dull."

[17] It is curious that Allardyce Nicoll ("The Dramatic Portrait of George Chapman," *PQ*, XLI [Jan. 1962], 218) finds *Westward Ho* to be "a wholly unsatirical play."

[18] Alfred Harbage, *Shakespeare and the Rival Traditions* (New York, 1952), p. 196.

[19] The quote is from Pierce, p. 131. Investigations by Stoll, Hunt, and Rupert Brooke (*John Webster and the Elizabethan Drama* [London, 1917]) demonstrate that the *Ho* plays are essentially Dekker's. Peter B. Murray, using as his test the occurrence of has, hath, doth, I'm, 'em, and ha', comes to the conclusion that Webster wrote about 40% of each play, but also asserts that "most of the events and the structure of plots may well be Dekker's." "The Collaboration of Dekker and Webster in *Northward Ho* and *Westward Ho*," *PBSA*, LVI (1962), 485.

[20] Stoll, p. 80.

[21] The attitudes of Bellamont and Dekker are so close in this respect that a further argument is provided against the view that Bellamont is a caricature of Chapman. Bellamont is, as Allardyce Nicoll asserts, a full-length portrait of Chapman which need not have disturbed him.

[22] George R. Price, "The Shares of Middleton and Dekker in a Collaborated Play," *Papers of the Michigan Academy of Science, Arts and Letters*, XXX (1944), 613.

[23] Richard H. Barker. *Thomas Middleton* (New York, 1958), p. 76.

[24] A. H. Bullen, *The Works of Thomas Middleton* (London, 1885–86), I, xxxcii.

[25] Bowers, III, 8.

[26] Bowers, III, 372.

[27] Even modern readers find them more distasteful than most characters in drama. "In *The Virgin Martyr*, where we have the odious servants, Hircius and Spungius, it is generally believed that the parts of the play in which they appear are due to Dekker, not to Massinger, whose other works present nothing so disgusting." A. H. Cruickshank, *Philip Massinger* (New York, 1902), p. 62.

[28] In the light of Dekker's entire output, it is difficult to believe Alfred Harbage's contention that "Dekker clung tenaciously to his principles no matter when, for whom, or with whom he wrote." "The Mystery of Perkin Warbeck," *Studies in the English Renaissance Drama* (New York, 1959), 140. It is also difficult to accept Marie Therese Jones-Davies' premise in her two exhaustive and competent volumes on Dekker that what he wrote is primarily the expression of his own individuality. Her admiration for his eclecticism never leads her to suspect his hack tendencies. *Un Peintre de la Vie Londonienne: Thomas Dekker* (Paris, 1958).

CHAPTER 4

[1] Ben Jonson, *Every Man in His Humour,* Prologue, 11. 21–24, in *Ben Jonson,* eds. C. H. Herford and Percy & Evelyn Simpson (Oxford, 1925–51), 11 vols. (Subsequent references will be made to this text.)

[2] The argument that Volpone's lust *does* alienate the audience is presented by Alexander H. Sackton, *Rhetoric as a Dramatic Language in Ben Jonson* (New York, 1948), p. 140, and is supported by Allan C. Dessen, *"Volpone* and Late Morality Tradition," *MLQ* (Dec. 1964).

[3] M. C. Bradbrook, *The Growth and Structure of Elizabethan Comedy* (London, 1955), p. 145.

[4] Wallace A. Bacon, "The Magnetic Field: The Structure of Jonson's Comedies," *Huntington Library Quarterly,* XIX (Feb. 1956), 137.

[5] Harry Levin, "Jonson's Metempsychosis," *PQ,* XXII (1943), 237.

[6] Herford and Simpson, II, 105.

[7] E. A. Horsman, ed. *Bartholomew Fair* (Cambridge, Mass., 1960), p. xx.

[8] Ray L. Heffner, "Unifying Symbols in the Comedy of Ben Jonson," in *Shakespeare's Contemporaries,* eds. Max Bluestone and Norman Rabkin (New Jersey, 1961), p. 199.

[9] John J. Enck, *Jonson and the Comic Truth* (Madison, 1957), p. 196.

[10] Richard Levin, discussing the play's structure, does not confront the underworld as a symbol, hoping to "counteract what seems to be a recent tendency to romanticize and to magnify the importance of the 'Bartholmew-birds.' " "The Structure of *Bartholomew Fair,*" *PMLA,* LXXX (June 1965), 178. For Levin "the actual movement of the play" does not justify the views of Bacon, Barish, and Enck that Ursula and company have a symbolic function. But surely a play is more than "movement"; a structural analysis, effective as Levin's is, does not necessarily deal with what can be called the play's issues or values.

[11] Jonas A. Barish, *Ben Jonson and the Language of Prose Comedy* (Cambridge, Mass., 1960), p. 225.

[12] *Discoveries,* Herford and Simpson, VIII, 588.

[13] Freda L. Townsend, *Apologie for Bartholmew Fayre* (New York, 1947), p. 82.

[14] Herford and Simpson, II, 177.

[15] Harry Levin, ed. *Ben Jonson: Selected Works* (New York, 1938), p. 11.

[16] John Palmer, *Ben Jonson* (New York, 1934), p. 187.

CHAPTER 5

[1] It is beyond the purposes of this study to detail the various aspects of this reflection. Two discussions of Shakespeare's use of the different plots in *A Midsummer Night's Dream* can be found in: John Palmer,

Comic Characters of Shakespeare (London, 1961), pp. 92–109. E. K. Chambers, *Shakespeare: A Survey* (London, 1925), pp. 77–87.

[2] Caroline Spurgeon finds more moon references in *A Midsummer Night's Dream* than in any other Shakespeare play. *Shakespeare's Imagery* (Cambridge, 1952), p. 259.

[3] In *Henry VI, Part 2* there is a division of society between the court world and the rebel world of Jack Cade, but Shakespeare does not fully exploit the Cade world as reflector, as he does the Bottom world in *A Midsummer Night's Dream.*

[4] William Shakespeare, *Richard II*, Act V, scene 3, 11. 5–12, in *The Complete Works of William Shakespeare,* ed. Hardin Craig (New York, 1951). (Subsequent references will be made to this text.)

[5] J. Dover Wilson, *The Fortunes of Falstaff* (New York, 1944), p. 20.

[6] E. M. W. Tillyard, *Shakespeare's History Plays* (London, 1959).

[7] Derek Traversi, *Shakespeare from Richard II to Henry V* (Stanford, 1957).

[8] Traversi, p. 10.

[9] It is encouraging that Leo Kirschbaum, writing independently, has also emphasized that thieving is Falstaff's vocation. "The Demotion of Falstaff," *PQ,* XLI (Jan. 1962), 58–60.

[10] G. Wilson Knight, M. C. Bradbrook, and Roy Battenhouse hold this view.

G. Wilson Knight, *The Wheel of Fire* (Oxford, 1930).

M. C. Bradbrook, "Authority, Truth, and Justice in *Measure for Measure,*" *RES,* XVII (1941), pp. 385-399.

Roy Battenhouse, "*Measure for Measure* and the Christian Doctrine of Atonement," *PMLA* (1946), 1029-59.

[11] Bertrand Evans, *Shakespeare's Comedies* (Oxford, 1960), p. 237.

[12] G. Wilson Knight, *The Crown of Life* (Oxford, 1947), p. 112.

CONCLUSION

[1] This view of Dekker is essentially contrary to the comments on Dekker's gentleness and understanding which one finds in the work of most critics of Dekker. Obvious examples are T. S. Eliot's "Dekker is all sentiment" (*Selected Essays* [New York, 1932], p. 146) and M. T. Jones-Davies' "La poesie et la jovialite qui penetrent l'oeuvre parlent aux sentiments et aux aspirations, plutot qu'a l'intelligence des lecteurs ou des spectateurs. Souvent elles reposent sur une profonde sympathie humaine. Cette sympathie intuitive est si naturelle a Dekker qu'elle influe sur l'eclairage de sa peinture." (*Un Peintre de la Vie Londonienne: Thomas Dekker,* II, 330.) These and similar statements concerning the "gentle" Dekker are discussed in the present writer's article, "Thomas Dekker: A Partial Reappraisal," *SEL,* VI (Spring, 1966), pp. 263–277. The article contains material found in Chapter 3 of this book.

Texts of the Plays Discussed in Chapter 2

Albion, Knight—Six Anonymous Plays, ed. John S. Farmer. London, 1905.

All for Money—Thomas Lupton. *All for Money.* Tudor Facsimile Texts, 1910.

Cambises—The Origin of the English Drama, ed. Thomas Hawkins. Oxford, 1773.

Chester Plays—The Chester Plays, ed. Hermann Deimling. Early English Text Society. London, 1892.

Common Conditions—Five Anonymous Plays, ed. John S. Farmer. London, 1908.

Digby Plays—The Digby Plays, ed. F. J. Furnivall. Early English Text Society. London, 1896.

Godly Queen Hester—Six Anonymous Plays, ed. John S. Farmer. London, 1905.

Hyckescorner—Specimens of the Pre-Shakespearean Drama, ed. John M. Manly. Boston, 1897.

John the Evangelist—John the Evangelist, ed. W. W. Greg. Malone Society Reprints, 1907.

King John—Specimens of the Pre-Shakespearean Drama, ed. John M. Manly. Boston, 1897.

Knack to Know a Knave—Old English Plays, ed. W. C. Hazlitt. London, 1874.

Liberality and Prodigality—The Contention between Liberality and Prodigality, ed. W. W. Greg. Malone Society Reprints, 1913.

*Life and Repentaunce of Marie Magdalene—*Lewis Wager. *The Life and Repentaunce of Marie Magdalene,* ed. Frederic I. Carpenter. Chicago, 1902.

Like Will to Like—The Dramatic Writings of Ulpian Fulwell, ed. John S. Farmer. London, 1906.

*Longer Thou Livest—*William Wager. *The Longer Thou Livest, the More Fool Thou Art.* Tudor Facsimile Texts, 1910.

*Magnyfycence—*John Skelton. *Magnyfycence,* ed. Robert L. Ramsay. Early English Text Society. London, 1906.

Mankind—The Macro Plays, ed. F. J. Furnivall. Early English Text Society. London, 1904.

Marriage between Wit and Wisdom—Five Anonymous Plays, ed. John S. Farmer. London, 1908.

Mind, Will, and Understanding—The Macro Plays, ed. F. J. Furnivall. Early English Text Society. London, 1904.

Misogonus—Six Anonymous Plays, ed. John S. Farmer. London, 1905.

Mundus et Infans—Specimens of the Pre-Shakespearean Drama, ed. John M. Manly. Boston, 1897.

Nature—"Lost" Tudor Plays, ed. John S. Farmer. London, 1907.

Nature of the Four Elements—Six Anonymous Plays, ed. John S. Farmer. London, 1905.

Nice Wanton—Specimens of the Pre-Shakespearean Drama, ed. John M. Manly. Boston, 1897.

Secunda Pastorum—The Towneley Plays, eds. George England

and A. W. Pollard. Early English Text Society. London,
1897.

Three Ladies of London—Old English Plays, ed. W. C. Hazlitt.
London, 1874.

Towneley Plays—The Towneley Plays, eds. George England and
A. W. Pollard. Early English Text Society. London, 1897.

Wealth and Health—Wealth and Health, ed. W. W. Greg.
Malone Society Reprints, 1907.

York Plays—York Plays, ed. Lucy T. Smith. Oxford, 1885.

Youth—Six Anonymous Plays, ed. John S. Farmer. London,
1905.

Index